The Economics of the Audiovisual Industry

DOI: 10.1057/9781137378477.0001

Other Palgrave Pivot titles

Piero Formica: **The Role of Creative Ignorance: Portraits of Path Finders and Path Creators**

James Carson: **The Columbian Covenant: Race and the Writing of American History**

Tomasz Kamusella: **Creating Languages in Central Europe during the Last Millennium**

Imad A. Moosa and Kelly Burns: **Demystifying the Meese–Rogoff Puzzle**

Kazuhiko Togo and GVC Naidu (editors): **Building Confidence in East Asia: Maritime Conflicts, Interdependence and Asian Identity Thinking**

Aylish Wood: **Software, Animation and the Moving Image: What's in the Box?**

Mo Jongryn (editor): **MIKTA, Middle Powers, and New Dynamics of Global Governance: The G20's Evolving Agenda**

Holly Jarman: **The Politics of Trade and Tobacco Control**

Cruz Medina: **Reclaiming Poch@ Pop: Examining the Rhetoric of Cultural Deficiency**

David McCann: **From Protest to Pragmatism: The Unionist Government and North-South Relations from 1959–72**

Thijl Sunier and Nico Landman: **Transnational Turkish Islam: Shifting Geographies of Religious Activism and Community Building in Turkey and Europe**

Daria J. Kuss and Mark D. Griffiths: **Internet Addiction in Psychotherapy**

Elisa Giacosa: **Innovation in Luxury Fashion Family Business: Processes and Products Innovation as a Means of Growth**

Domagoj Hruška: **Radical Decision Making: Leading Strategic Change in Complex Organizations**

Bjørn Møller: **Refugees, Prisoners and Camps: A Functional Analysis of the Phenomenon of Encampment**

David Ralph: **Work, Family and Commuting in Europe: The Lives of Euro-commuters**

Emily F. Henderson: **Gender Pedagogy: Teaching, Learning and Tracing Gender in Higher Education**

Mihail Evans: **The Singular Politics of Derrida and Baudrillard**

Bryan Fanning and Andreas Hess: **Sociology in Ireland: A Short History**

Tom Watson (editor): **Latin American and Caribbean Perspectives on the Development of Public Relations: Other Voices**

Anshu Saxena Arora and Sabine Bacouël-Jentjens (editors): **Advertising Confluence: Transitioning the World of Marketing Communications into Social Movements**

Bruno Grancelli: **The Architecture of Russian Markets: Organizational Responses to Institutional Change**

Michael A. Smith, Kevin Anderson, Chapman Rackaway, and Alexis Gatson: **State Voting Laws in America: Voting Fraud, or Fraudulent Voters?**

Nicole Lindstrom: **The Politics of Europeanization and Post-Socialist Transformations**

Madhvi Gupta and Pushkar: **Democracy, Civil Society, and Health in India**

DOI: 10.1057/9781137378477.0001

palgrave▸pivot

The Economics of the Audiovisual Industry: Financing TV, Film and Web

Mario La Torre

Professor of Financial Markets and Intermediaries, University of Rome, Italy

Supported by the Italian Ministry of Culture – Cinema Division and Centro Sperimentale di Cinematografia

palgrave macmillan

DOI: 10.1057/9781137378477.0001

First published 2014 by
PALGRAVE MACMILLAN

Palgrave Macmillan in the UK is an imprint of Macmillan Publishers Limited, registered in England, company number 785998, of Houndmills, Basingstoke, Hampshire, RG21 6XS.

Palgrave Macmillan in the US is a division of St Martin's Press LLC, 175 Fifth Avenue, New York, NY 10010.

Palgrave Macmillan is the global academic imprint of the above companies and has companies and representatives throughout the world.

ISBN: 978-1-137-37848-4 EPUB
ISBN: 978-1-137-37847-7 PDF
ISBN: 978-1-137-37846-0 Hardback

This book is printed on paper suitable for recycling and made from fully managed and sustained forest sources. Logging, pulping and manufacturing processes are expected to conform to the environmental regulations of the country of origin.

A catalogue record for this book is available from the British Library.

A catalog record for this book is available from the Library of Congress.

www.palgrave.com/pivot

DOI: 10.1057/9781137378477

To Janet, my favourite moving image

DOI: 10.1057/9781137378477.0001

Contents

DOI: 10.1057/9781137378477.0001

List of Figures

DOI: 10.1057/9781137378477.0002

List of Tables

DOI: 10.1057/9781137378477.0003

Acknowledgements

This book has been published with the support of the "Centro Sperimentale di Cinematografia" and the Cinema Division of the Italian Ministry of Culture. A special thanks to Nicola Borrelli and Marcello Foti for believing in the project.

The author wishes to thank Cineconsulting Group and all its staff; to Barbara Bettelli and Gian Marco Committeri goes a sign of gratitude and friendship for the never-ending passionate discussions on many of the topics covered in the text.

The author is solely responsible for what is written.

DOI: 10.1057/9781137378477.0004

About the Author

Mario La Torre is Professor of Financial Markets and Intermediaries at the University of Rome "La Sapienza". His main research areas are banking and finance, ethical finance and impact finance, and audiovisual and art financing.

In the audiovisual industry he has played several institutional roles; he has been member of the Board of Directors of Cinecittà Holding and Counsellor of the Minister of Culture. He has been a lawmaker of the Italian Tax Credit Law for the audiovisual industry. He is currently counselling the Cinema Division of the Ministry of Culture. He is member of the Audiovisual Working Party of the Council of the European Union and member of the Scientific Advisor Board of Cineconsulting Group.

Mario La Torre is also member of the Board of the Italian National Body for Microcredit. He has been member of the Taskforce on Social Impact Investments established by the G7 countries and member of the consultative group for the definition of the Italian Microcredit Law. He is currently editor of the new Series "Palgrave Studies in Impact Finance".

His main international publications include "Microcredit Securitization" co-written with Mango F., in *Bank Performance, Risk and Securitisation*, Palgrave Macmillan, 2013; "Social Lending in Europe: Structures, Regulation and Pricing Models" co-written with Mango F., in *Crisis, Risk and Stability in Financial Markets*, Palgrave Macmillan, 2013; "Asset-Backed Securitization and Financial Stability:

DOI: 10.1057/9781137378477.0005

The Downgrading Delay Effect" co-written with Mango F., in *Banks Performance Risk and Firm Financing*, Palgrave Macmillan, 2011; "Banks in the Microfinance Market" co-written with Vento G., in *Frontiers of Banks in a Global Economy*, Palgrave Macmillan, 2008; "Agevolazioni fiscali per il cinema" co-written with Committeri G.M., *Quaderni Anica*, 2008; *Microfinance*, Palgrave Macmillan, 2006; *La Finanza del Cinema*, Bancaria Editrice, 2006.

DOI: 10.1057/9781137378477.0005

OPEN

1
Introduction

Abstract: *This book is not meant to be a report on the state of the art of the audiovisual industry, nor a survey of best practices and key players operating in the market, but a theoretical picture analysing the main economic and financial features of the audiovisual industry. The first section – Chapters 2 and 3 – describes the perimeter and the main features of the audiovisual industry; Chapters 4, 5 and 6 analyse the economics of the industry – mainly costs and revenues, pricing models and value of audiovisual firms; Chapters 7 and 8 explores audiovisual funding and the related risks; a financial platform for the audiovisual industry is proposed in Chapter 9, together with conclusions. In this perspective, the book represents a useful guide for professionals and producers, as well as for bankers, financial managers and academics.*

La Torre, Mario. *The Economics of the Audiovisual Industry: Financing TV, Film and Web.* Basingstoke: Palgrave Macmillan, 2014. DOI: 10.1057/9781137378477.0006.

A remarkable number of bankers and professionals working in finance still currently believe that the cultural industry is a high-risk market, as well as a low-profit one, with uncertain and unclear peculiarities. In other words, they are persuaded that culture should not be financed.

Considering the perspective of cultural industry, banks and financial intermediaries are perceived as interlocutors unable to understand the specific needs of the industry itself, even worse, unable to substitute short-term profits with a holistic perspective of finance, considering those medium- and long-term externalities created by cultural production.

In general, a lack of mutual knowledge, different priorities, a different language, as well as the different expertise of bankers and financial experts on one side and of players and cultural managers on the other side, have created a permanent shorting out between cultural industry and financial markets. Since this shorting out is self-supplied, changing the situation is very difficult. This happens for all creativity industries, audiovisual included.

Even though audiovisual sectors show a structure of market supply based upon more organized companies compared to other cultural industries, and they are also characterized by a higher management expertise, they have to face a crucial distance from the financial system. This phenomenon is easily noticeable in all European countries. Unlike the United States, the credit granted by the banking system to the audiovisual industry throughout the main countries of continental Europe currently represents a very small share of the total issued credit. Furthermore, a very small number of audiovisual companies are listed on the stock exchange, and very few firms have access to capital markets to attract funds from institutional or retail investors. Except for the USA, the financing of audiovisual industry is based upon internal financial resources, or supported by public funds. In Europe, for example, together with public funds, both at a national and local level, European financial resources intended to support culture – and indirectly SMEs and new technologies – are undeniably crucial for the industry.

However, audiovisual firms, especially in the European context, are struggling to achieve a corporate restructuring, as well as a change in financial management. The financial crisis and the decrease in public financial resources available have motivated European governments and institutions to implement new support mechanisms in order to foster public-private partnerships and to deal with market evolutions. Companies search for new organizational and productive models, in

DOI: 10.1057/9781137378477.0006

addition to new management strategies. The new challenges require the implementation of competitive strategies and a high degree of dynamism.

Such a goal cannot be achieved without the support of financial markets and intermediaries, in particular banks, which in time have always represented the first link among industrial sectors and the financial system, preliminary to stock exchange markets.

The interaction between audiovisual industry and financial markets cannot happen in a virtuous way in absence of a process of mutual knowledge.

Literature concerning the management of cultural industry is quite limited and mainly focussed on macro-economic variables and market dynamics, as well as strategic management and marketing. Financial management of cultural firms is almost unnoticed and appears to be well known only by a few managers and bankers, since they have acquired specific professional expertise in the industry. This circumstance does not foster cultural industry emancipation from public financial support, in particular from the subsidiary type.

The idea of writing this book rises from the need to create a systematic framework of economic and financial dynamics of the cultural industry. The study focuses on the audiovisual market, this being an important segment of cultural industry, as well as one of the most flexible, able to cope with the need of transformation and to deal with the challenges of new financial markets.

The book is not meant to be a report on the state of the art of the audiovisual industry, nor a survey of best practices and key players operating in the market. Rather, the market trend has inspired a theoretical reconstruction of the economics of the industry. The reading of the text, therefore, should not be given to research data, names and numbers, but rather to metabolize economic and financial models useful to work in the audiovisual sectors.

In this perspective, the book, analysing the main economic and financial features of the audiovisual industry, represents a useful guide for professionals and producers willing to interact with banks and financial intermediaries, as well as for bankers, financial managers and academics willing to acquire an in-depth knowledge of the audiovisual industry, embracing a tailor-made risk management approach.

Considering another point of view, the analysis of economic, financial and production dynamics of the audiovisual industry can make this

DOI: 10.1057/9781137378477.0006

book a useful guide also for policy makers, at a national and European level. It will be particularly advantageous for those who are committed to direct audiovisual finance towards market dynamics, in order to foster private-public partnerships.

In absence of a specific literature, the theoretical structure of the analysis is based upon the same used in financial and economic literature. The context of traditional theoretical references for the audiovisual industry represents the original contribution of the study and is the outcome of the author's professional and institutional experience.

Readers can imagine this book as based upon three units. The first section (Chapters 2 and 3) provides an outline of audiovisual industry. Chapter 2 explains the main determinants of the distance existing among the audiovisual industry and financial markets, highlighting the main drivers pushing the audiovisual towards a modern finance. Chapter 3 defines the perimeter of the audiovisual industry and describes the different types of audiovisual products, as well as the related audiovisual sectors.

The second section (Chapters 4, 5 and 6) concerns the economics of audiovisual production. In more detail, Chapter 4 analyses the main costs and revenues of audiovisual products, Chapter 5 proposes a pricing model for audiovisual products, while Chapter 6 provides a model for the estimation of the value of audiovisual firms.

Section 3 (Chapters 7 and 8) explores audiovisual funding and the related risks. Chapter 7 examines in detail the traditional financial model of audiovisual firms, while Chapter 8 describes the main financial techniques used by banks and financial intermediaries when they lend money to the audiovisual industry, also providing for a taxonomy of financial risks connected to audiovisual finance.

Conclusions are drawn in Chapter 9, proposing a market model focussed on the idea of a financial platform for the audiovisual industry.

DOI: 10.1057/9781137378477.0006

OPEN

2
Create Connections between Audiovisual and Finance

Abstract: *The finance of the audiovisual industry is essentially self-referential; therefore intermediaries and financial markets have a small influence. The chapter provides an insight on the explanations to the distance between the audiovisual industry and financial markets, considering both the perspective of audiovisual companies and financial intermediaries. It also analyses which reasons call for a deeper connection between audiovisual and financial industry and which requirements should be fulfilled to create a profitable and long-lasting interaction between audiovisual and financial markets.*

La Torre, Mario. *The Economics of the Audiovisual Industry: Financing TV, Film and Web.* Basingstoke: Palgrave Macmillan, 2014. DOI: 10.1057/9781137378477.0007.

2.1 Introduction

The audiovisual industry, as well as the entire cultural industry, has been experiencing for many years the outcomes of several innovations. Typically, they concern procedures, product policies and business strategies. The financial management of enterprises or single projects, on the contrary, is still on the margin of this enhancement process. Consequently, the finance of the audiovisual industry – and in broader terms of the cultural industry – is essentially self-referential; therefore, intermediaries and financial markets have a small influence. This peculiarity can be noticed at an international level, with few exceptions, including the USA, and it is particularly evident in European countries. Several studies and surveys have confirmed this evidence[1].

Why? What is the explanation for the distance among financial markets, intermediaries and audiovisual companies? What reasons would explain a deeper connection between the audiovisual and financial industries? What requirements should be fulfilled to create a profitable and a long-lasting connection? It is worth answering these questions if we want to foster the shift of audiovisual industry, as well as the entire cultural production, from a state of domestic handcrafted market to an industrial international dimension. This chapter provides an insight on the explanations about the distance between the audiovisual industry and financial markets, considering both the perspective of audiovisual companies and financial intermediaries.

In the light of the above-mentioned topics, the positive possible outcomes of an inversion of the trend are described, as well as with reference to the development of an audiovisual financial market.

2.2 The distance between audiovisual and finance: the concerns of audiovisual firms

The audiovisual industry and, in general, the cultural industry, are characterized by an evident fear (Figure 2.1): the access of financial intermediaries to the market would allow them to create a financial seigniorage on artistic production, transforming the cultural industry into a mere shooting ground for the search of new clients and new business opportunities.

DOI: 10.1057/9781137378477.0007

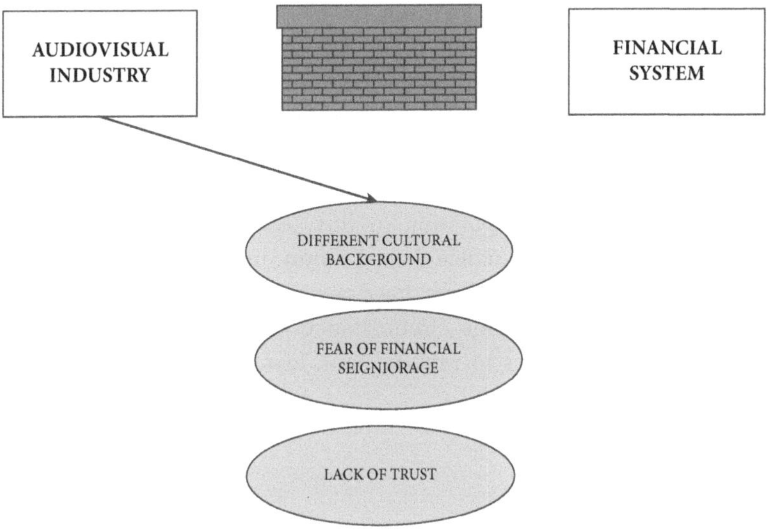

FIGURE 2.1 *The wall between audiovisual and finance: the concerns of audiovisual firms*

The cultural and linguistic shorting out created by audiovisual players' backgrounds, very different from those of finance professionals, has made misunderstandings, increasing the distance between the two realities. The above-mentioned issue is confirmed by a study commissioned by the European Commission[2], surveying 2,861 firms operating in the cultural industry: in the period of observation, only 38% of total cultural firms and 53% of total audiovisual firms involved in the survey contacted a bank to search for external finance; 67% of cultural firms and 74% of audiovisual firms approached a Government body. About 30% of cultural firms and 29% of audiovisual firms were convinced that contacting a bank is a waste of time; 32% of cultural firms and 48% of audiovisual firms had the perception that banks do not understand their business.

The distance between the audiovisual industry and finance is also due to the peculiarities of the audiovisual industry financial cycle. Sources of finance for the production of an audiovisual work can be identified, theoretically, both in internal and external financial resources. The first type includes equity, personal resources and rights of exploitation pre-sales

DOI: 10.1057/9781137378477.0007

on different markets, as well as funds from co-production agreements. The second type concerns public financial support – at a local, national and European level – also including all resources from private investors and financial markets (Figure 2.2).

Audiovisual companies deal with their structural need for financial resources mostly by rights of exploitation pre-sale and achieving public financial support. Firms operating in this sector prefer to substitute market finance with a finance based upon internal resources and on government subsidies, which have acquired the status of private investments "surrogates". This circumstance has reduced the urgency for audiovisual companies to require bank loans and to access capital markets.

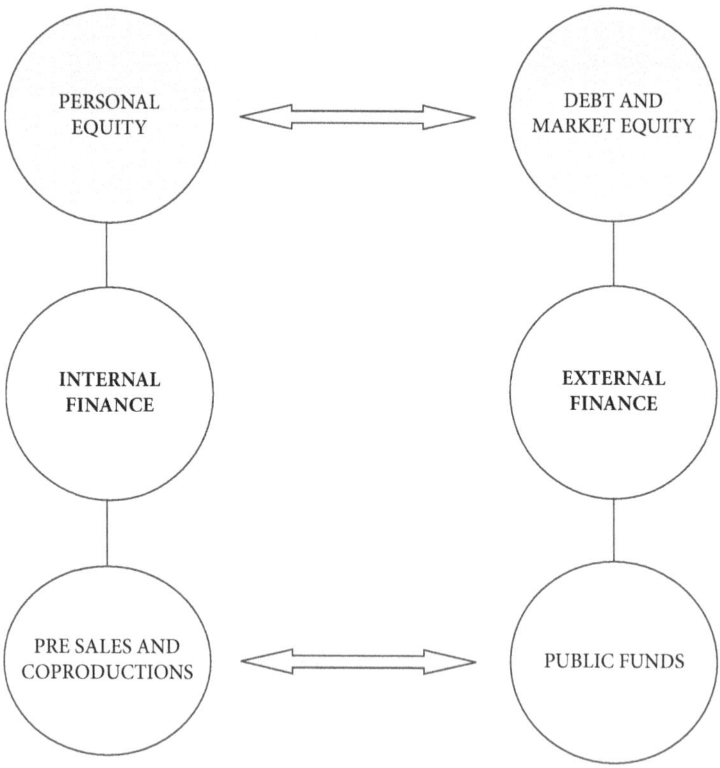

FIGURE 2.2 *Financial resources of the audiovisual sector*

DOI: 10.1057/9781137378477.0007

According to the cited IDEA (2013) study, business revenues and subsidies are the two most important financial resources for audiovisual firms and, in general, for cultural industry. This is consistent with the outcomes of other studies. The HKU survey reports that 56% of the cultural firms involved in the interview indicate self-financing as the most important financial resource. Only 12% indicate bank loans as the most important financial resource[3]. The KEA study confirms that self-financing is the basic financial resource, followed by retained profits: 61% of firms have never benefited from external finance[4].

Public financial support seems to be very important to start the funding process: according to KEA (2010 a), 59% of firms get access to public funds (57% tax incentives); on the contrary, public financing usually covers a small percentage of total production budget leaving producers with a significant gap financing.

2.3 The distance between audiovisual and finance: the concerns of financial intermediaries

Banks and other financial intermediaries have to deal with a misleading attitude in approaching the audiovisual industry. Except in the USA, very few collaborations have been developed upon the presumption to apply to the audiovisual industry the same financial support, analysis and risk management techniques used for other industrial sectors.

Several causes can explain the caution financial intermediaries have preferred to keep, more or less voluntarily, in their investments in the audiovisual industry. Those reasons refer to psychological and cultural aspects, to the nature of firms operating in the industry, to their balance sheet and to business peculiarities (Figure 2.3).

With reference to psychological and cultural determinants, besides the very well-known concern of stressing the cultural goal to the detriment of economic and financial requirements, it is also worth considering the belief that culture is a high-risk sector. According to IDEA (2013), 42% of cultural firms and 50% of audiovisual firms declare that banks have rejected their loan applications because the investment was considered too risky. Financial intermediaries' poor knowledge of cultural production dynamics, as well as of cultural industry economics, does not foster an objective evaluation of cultural and audiovisual projects. The production and the distribution of cultural products is a peculiar activity, and

DOI: 10.1057/9781137378477.0007

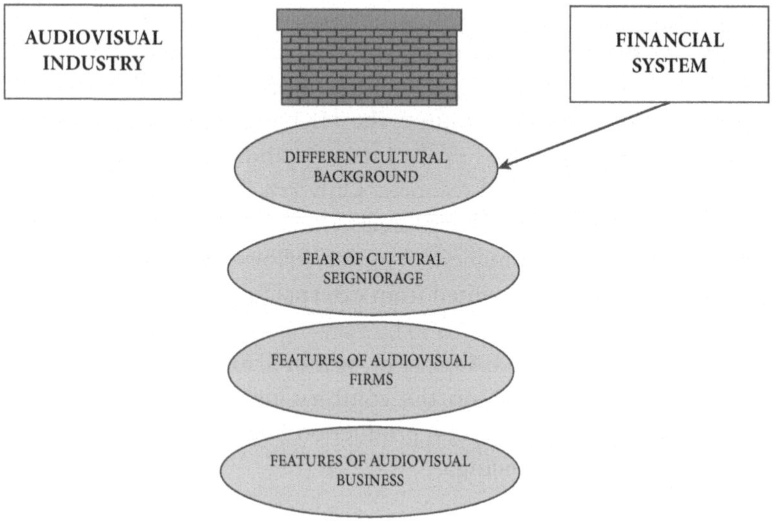

FIGURE 2.3 *The wall between audiovisual and finance: the concerns of financial intermediaries*

this makes such business hardly conceivable and hardly associable to other industries: lending money to a museum, or financing the production of a film, is not the same as granting credit to any other type of business.

Also intermediaries with a good knowledge of the audiovisual industry – and of the cultural industry in general – have to deal with many crucial issues.

Firstly, many criticisms concern market structure, that is to say the nature and the peculiarities of firms. The whole cultural industry, and the audiovisual industry in particular, is characterized by firms with a weak organizational structure; small dimensions, small number of employees and often non-profit oriented missions are the main causes. According to IDEA (2013), almost 30% of cultural organizations are one-person business entities, about 20% have no legal structure and 37% are non-profit organizations. Looking specifically at the audiovisual industry, over half of the firms in the study sample have 1 to 4 employees, 15% have no legal structure and 20% are non-profit organizations. The majority of audiovisual firms (51%) falls in the category of "less than 5 employees".

These features also affect the efficiency of cultural and audiovisual firms. The management of most cultural firms still does not prove to

DOI: 10.1057/9781137378477.0007

be efficient and transparent, and therefore it does not allow financial intermediaries and investors to complete an accurate evaluation of the credit rating of the borrowers. According to Clayton & Mason, only 36% of cultural firms declare to prepare formal business plans, while 35% use no formal ones and 29% have no business plans at all. These results are confirmed by the HKU survey, which shows that 75% of cultural firms make their own business plans and only 20% use professional consultancy services to approach banks and financial intermediaries. IDEA (2013) demonstrates that there is a strict connection between the ability to prepare a business plan and the size of the firm: only 20% of cultural firms with zero employees and 40% of firms with less than five employees (the majority of audiovisual firms) have a three-year business plan. As confirmed by Burrows and Ussher, this results in being one of the main obstacles in accessing external financial resources and, in general, in the interaction with banks and financial intermediaries[5].

Furthermore, it is also necessary to point out a wide underestimation of firms' equity, as well as their difficulties in providing real guarantees as possible funding collaterals. According to IDEA (2013), 38% of cultural firms and 45% of audiovisual firms declare that banks have rejected their loan applications because they could not, or refused to fulfil, collateral requirements.

Many criticalities concern the nature of business itself. Audiovisual products are often distributed in domestic markets, and this decreases potential revenues. Moreover, the estimation of audiovisual products is quite complex, since this mostly depends on audience appreciation and on the emotional experiences it is able to provide. Therefore, it is difficult to measure it *ex ante* since it cannot be defined based on objective quantitative parameters. Finally, public funding granted to audiovisual companies as non-recoupable financial support creates many constrains to pricing policies and intermediary profitability.

These are among the main reasons for the small amount of private funding granted to the cultural industry – and in particular to the audiovisual industry.

In most cases the audiovisual industry can benefit from short-/medium-term loans, granted to cover a financial gap, often provided based upon pre-sale rights contracts. According to the IDEA (2013) survey, 33% of loans granted to cultural firms show an average maturity of less than 1 year (66% less than three years); the percentage is equal to 26% for audiovisual firms (64% less than three years). Also the amount

DOI: 10.1057/9781137378477.0007

of loans agreed on is quite low, on average from 30,000 to 70,000 euros. Concerning the audiovisual industry, those amounts are more relevant, varying from 1.5 to 10 million euros. The explanation can be identified in a higher simplicity for bankers to finance audiovisual companies granting loans secured with pre-sales contracts.

2.4 The determinants for a financial development of the audiovisual industry

What causes can justify, considering the current context, an envisaged connection between audiovisual and finance? What is changing?

During the last few years many criticalities of the financial model adopted by the audiovisual industry have undoubtedly arisen. This model represents the milestone upon which the entire audiovisual industry has based its own survival and development since the post-war years. The recent financial crisis has generated two negative effects: the first one concerning internal financial resources, the second involving public funding.

Changes in trend of the economic cycle have caused an evident decrease in advertising incomes for TV broadcasters. It has negatively affected not only TV companies' balance sheets, but also other players of the audiovisual industry. The financial crisis has also imposed narrower boundaries on public expenditure. In the European Union, the fulfilment of the Stability and Growth Pact requirements has emphasized the need of Member States to reduce public contribution rates intended to support welfare state; cultural industries – primarily the audiovisual one – suffered from this situation.

Firms involved in the audiovisual industry have had to deal with a double financial criticality: with reference to internal sources of funds, it has meant a decrease in advertising incomes; regarding external financial resources, it has meant a reduction in public funding. A partial growth in the number of international co-productions has been the only positive outcome against the gap generated by the new context. The financial stress due to this context is risking to affect audiovisual firms' balance sheets (Figure 2.4).

A wider opening to financial markets, supported by a policy oriented to development of those potentialities still unrevealed by rights

DOI: 10.1057/9781137378477.0007

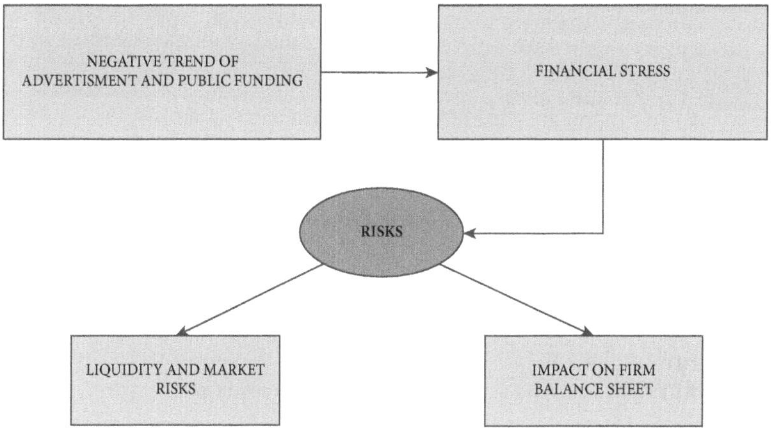

FIGURE 2.4 *The urgency for a new funding process of audiovisual firms*

exploitation markets, both at a national and at an international level, becomes a necessary path.

The existence of a potential market for private finance is also confirmed by the survey conducted by IDEA, which estimates that, in Europe, the financing gap in the cultural industry, considering a seven-year period (2014–2020), ranges from 8 to 13.4 billion, depending on different scenarios[6].

A new financial network for the audiovisual industry is not only necessary, but also justified by a relevant potential demand, which appoints private finance for the task of providing the necessary coverage to structural financial need of firms active in the industry (Figure 2.5).

Actually, the access to finance would represent for audiovisual companies a chance to enter two different types of market: credit market and capital market (Figure 2.6).

The first one, more traditional, assures bank loans and financial intermediaries support. The second type is related to securitization processes experienced by capital markets. Debt securities, equity instruments and shares are the correspondent financial tools, while financial intermediaries and other institutional investors are to be considered principal investors; private and retail customers will play a less crucial role.

However, in the lack of an effective action by policy makers and market players, it is difficult to envisage a path for a virtuous interaction between

DOI: 10.1057/9781137378477.0007

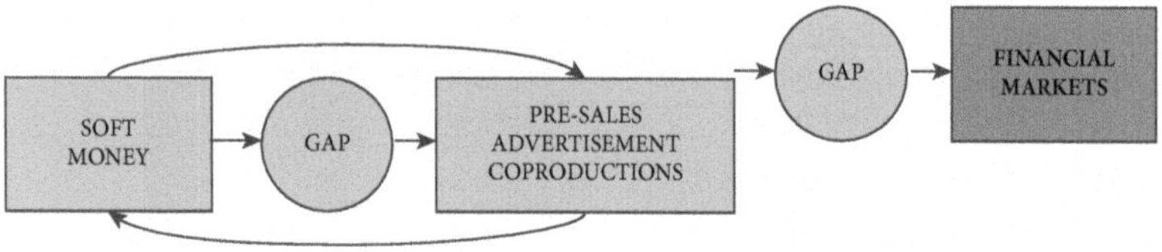

FIGURE 2.5 *Towards a sustainable funding process of the audiovisual firms*

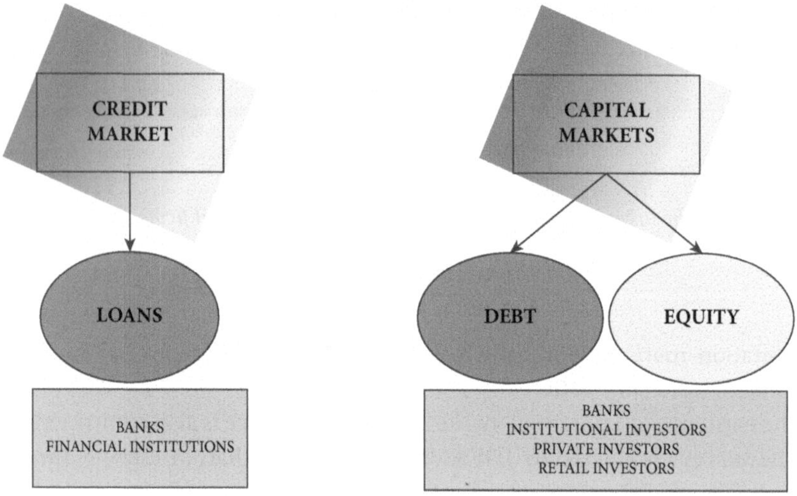

FIGURE 2.6 *Sources of private finance for the audiovisual firms*

financial markets and the audiovisual industry. According to the IDEA survey (2013), 62% of cultural firms have affirmed they would not apply for a bank loan in the upcoming six months. This is clear evidence that something must be done in order to reverse the trend.

Notes

1 Among others: Clayton & Mason 2006, HKU 2010, Kea 2010 a, IDEA Consult 2012 and 2013.
2 IDEA Consult, 2013.
3 HKU 2010.

DOI: 10.1057/9781137378477.0007

4 KEA 2010a.
5 Burrows and Ussher 2011.
6 IDEA Consult, 2013.

DOI: 10.1057/9781137378477.0007

OPEN

3 Defining the Audiovisual Industry

Abstract: *This chapter defines the perimeter of the audiovisual industry based on theoretical approaches adopted in literature, as well as the regulatory one used by policy makers. The perimeter of the audiovisual industry will be defined also with reference to classifications based upon statistics and accounting needs. Implementing an empirical approach, the chapter defines the different audiovisual sectors based on the intersection of three variables: the nature of audiovisual products, production process and distribution dynamics. In accordance to these variables, it is possible to identify three macro-sectors: television, cinema and web. For each sector, this chapter will explore the peculiarities of the main audiovisual products.*

La Torre, Mario. *The Economics of the Audiovisual Industry: Financing TV, Film and Web*. Basingstoke: Palgrave Macmillan, 2014. DOI: 10.1057/9781137378477.0008.

 DOI: 10.1057/9781137378477.0008

3.1 Introduction

A satisfactory analysis of the audiovisual industry requires defining the perimeter of the different audiovisual markets. Markets identification implies an in-depth knowledge of specific products circulating in those markets. With reference to the audiovisual industry, the definition of the typical product is more complex than it could be for other industries. Indeed, the approach cannot focus only on technical and commercial features. Besides a mere technical aspect, that is to say the definition of the product as a combination of sounds and images, it is worth considering the deep connection existing between audiovisual and cultural product. That is the reason why the audiovisual industry is considered as a subset of the cultural one.

This chapter defines the perimeter of the audiovisual industry based on theoretical approaches adopted in literature, as well as the regulatory one used by policy makers. The perimeter of the audiovisual industry will be defined also with reference to classifications based upon statistics and accounting needs. Implementing an empirical approach, the chapter defines audiovisual sectors based on the intersection of three variables: the nature of audiovisual products, production process and distribution dynamics. In accordance to these variables, it is possible to identify three macro-sectors: television, cinema and web. For each sector, this chapter will explore the peculiarities of the main audiovisual products.

3.2 The perimeter of the audiovisual industry

Theoretical approach to cultural industry

All attempts to find a taxonomic definition for cultural industries have different roots, but they all share the same common need: the measurement of the actual value of cultural industry, as well as its impacts in economic and social terms[1]. This purpose can be achieved considering different perspectives (Table 3.1).

Traditionally, literature has always focused on the "intrinsic value" of culture and, therefore, on its ability to communicate moral and ideological messages, studying impacts in terms of aesthetic excellence and individual enjoyment – associated with the concept of beauty or moral

DOI: 10.1057/9781137378477.0008

TABLE 3.1 *The value of cultural industry*

INTRINSIC VALUE	INSTITUTIONAL VALUE	MICROECONOMIC VALUE
Focused on the impacts of culture on personal and social welfare, mainly measured by individual enjoyment and aesthetic excellence.	*Focused on the impacts of culture on direct and indirect macroeconomic effects, mainly on the labour market and tourism sector.*	*Focused on the value of cultural products, mainly measured by the willingness of the public to pay for it. It is also used to value a cultural firm.*

improvement and spiritual development – and, in general, in terms of social welfare[2].

Another branch of the research has been investigating the "economic value" of culture. In this field, two approaches can be followed: the first one is focused on the "institutional value" of culture and analyses impacts associated to macroeconomic effects generated by cultural production; the second one is aimed at investigating the "micro-economic value", meant as people's preferences expressed by price or willingness to pay[3].

Literature based upon the "institutional value" of culture has inspired the current definition of cultural industry, frequently used by governments and institutions while undertaking a cost-benefits analysis of public financial support to be granted to the cultural industry. The "micro-economic value" has been less explored by scholars and policy makers. This perspective is deeply connected to the economic value of cultural products, as well as to the cultural firm itself. The underestimation of this perspective has caused the current distance between cultural industries and financial markets: investments are inspired by expectations and measures of the risk-return factors inherent to the projects, as well as the rating of the company that benefits from the financing. Therefore, those analyses do not consider macroeconomic impacts, nor cultural or intrinsic value.

In this perspective, the philosophical discussion about culture is not relevant – though very interesting by the way – on the contrary, theories based upon economic value and focused on a mere empirical approach are crucial at this point of our study. It is then quite useful to anticipate that the inclusion of audiovisual within the cultural industry is mostly due to theories inspired by "institutional value", more than the "intrinsic value" of culture.

DOI: 10.1057/9781137378477.0008

The perimeter of cultural industry

The need to measure the impact of cultural production, both in terms of social dimensions and economic nature, has persuaded academics to explore the taxonomic features of cultural sectors.

Prior to every kind of analysis, it is necessary to identify those sectors and activities to include in the perimeter of cultural industry. Theories based on the economic value, in particular those connected to the "institutional value", do not exclude cultural aspects; however, they link the "intrinsic value" to the conception of creativity, including in the perimeter of cultural industry, both cultural and macroeconomic features. Consequently, a fundamental difference between the European and the American approach must be stressed: while the first one is focused on the creative industry, the second one concentrates on the creativity of single employees. The evolution of the interpretation guided both approaches to the achievement of an expanded vision of cultural industry's perimeter. According to the European approach, the perspective is based on the evidence that products fulfilling primary functions can contain elements of creativity. The American perspective is based upon the idea that creative professionals work also in other industrial sectors, not necessarily included in cultural industry. In both approaches, anyway, creativity is linked to the construct of intellectual property.

This overview is synthesized in the definition of creative industry provided by the *UK Department of Culture Media and Sport* (DCMS) in 1998: creative industries "have their origin in individual creativity, skill and talent and have a potential for wealth and job creation through the generation and exploitation of intellectual property". Whichever is the aspect we are focussing on, the importance of the industry, or the role of employees, the creativity rate of a product is defined – mainly – as the ability of the product itself to be the outcome and to represent the expression of the originality, talent and technique of its creator. This does not depend on the economic value; nonetheless, the economic exploitation of the product does not prevent the presence of a creative feature. The originality of this approach is based upon its ability to combine cultural and economic value. It is possible owing to the conception of creativity. Every product characterized by a creative feature, even with primary functions and having an economic value, can be considered as a cultural product; therefore, the productive sector it belongs to is the cultural one. This explains how, and why, along with sectors historically considered to

DOI: 10.1057/9781137378477.0008

be cultural – such as the performing arts and visual arts – are now also included in the cultural industry sectors such as fashion or design.

According to this perspective, the 2006 KEA study[4] distinguishes between "cultural sectors" and "creative sectors". "Cultural sectors" are split into "core art fields" and "cultural industries". "Core art fields" are non-industrial sectors producing non-reproducible goods to be consumed on the spot; "cultural industries" include industrial sectors producing cultural products in order to achieve a mass reproduction. "Creative industries" include sectors producing non-cultural goods with creative input.

In 2010, also the European Commission, in the *Green Paper on Culture*[5], followed an extensive approach:

> Cultural industries are those industries producing and distributing goods or services which at the time they are developed are considered to have a specific attribute, use or purpose which embodies or conveys cultural expressions, irrespective of the commercial value they may have. Besides the traditional arts sectors (performing arts, visual arts, cultural heritage – including the public sector), they include film, DVD and video, television and radio, video games, new media, music, books and press... Creative industries are those industries which use culture as an input and have a cultural dimension, although their outputs are mainly functional. They include architecture and design, which integrate creative elements into wider processes, as well as subsectors such as graphic design, fashion design or advertising. At a more peripheral level, many other industries rely on content production for their own development and are therefore to some extent interdependent with CCIs. They include among others tourism and the new technologies sector.

It is the potential presence of creative aspects in planning and development stages that allows the inclusion of a specific sector in the creative industry. For traditional cultural sectors, the creative element is represented by originality and unicity, as well as by the absence of a primary instrumental function. For example, in a theatre the creative element is characterized by the originality and the unicity of the performance, which is not aimed at achieving any instrumental function. However, in a few sectors, products can be linked to basic functions but can include a creative element. The architectural project of an auditorium, for example, has a specific function: it has to create a space in which to listen to music and can be developed with or without an original creative element. A canvas can be used to paint a picture or to create a dress: the painting is the result of a creative element, since normally it is original and

DOI: 10.1057/9781137378477.0008

cannot be reproduced; the dress, normally, doesn't incorporate a creative element, since it can be reproduced in series with an industrial process. But if it is a tailored dress, it cannot be reproduced, because it is original, therefore acquiring an unusual creative element. This approach allows the inclusion in the cultural sector of those hybrid products, which can have an original, or a creative and unique, element. The theoretical weakness of this approach is caused by the circumstance that traditional cultural sectors can generate non-creative products. When a painting is the reproduction of another one – and therefore it can be reproduced – the creative element disappears, unless it can be identified in an original reproduction technique.

With reference to the outcomes of the KEA and European Commission studies, the UNESCO approach adds a further detail. In 2009 UNESCO, revising its framework of cultural statistics from 1986, suggested a broader definition of cultural industry[6]. The new classification considers not only cultural products and business products with cultural elements but also cross-sector products, linked to cultural ones. The main news concern: (a) the inclusion of the sector "design and creative services" among cultural sectors; and (b) the inclusion of cross-sector areas aimed at being functional for the production and the distribution of products in several cultural sectors (*intangible cultural heritage* – considered "merely cultural" – *archiving and preserving, education and training, equipment and support materials* – considered "partially cultural"), represented by "activities that may have a cultural character, but their main component is not cultural".

In brief, the expanded and modern vision of cultural industry is based upon a paramount aspect: creativity. By merging different approaches, it is possible to build up a taxonomy of cultural industry that would be composed of three levels: strong culturality, hybrid culturality and a functional culturality (Table 3.2).

The strongly cultural sectors encompass those products acknowledged as traditional, characterized by an original creative element, as well as by their unicity and the absence of instrumental functions (such as *performing arts, visual arts, cultural heritage, books and press, music, radio, film, television, DVD, video, video games* and *new media*).

The hybrid-cultural sectors include two peculiar types of products and sectors: those that are usually characterized by instrumental functions, but that can also involve creative features, being almost impossible to reproduce (i.e., *architecture, design, fashion* and *advertising*). This sector

DOI: 10.1057/9781137378477.0008

TABLE 3.2 *The perimeter of cultural industry*

STRONG CULTURALITY	HYBRID CULTURALITY	FUNCTIONAL CULTURALITY
Includes products, and correlated sectors, expression of original creativity, without any instrumental function, which may be considered as prototypes.	*Includes products, and related sectors, which: a) perform an instrumental function but may be inspired by a creative component and may be considered as prototypes b) are deeply connected to a cultural function because they perform a recreation and an entertainment function*	*Includes products, and correlated sectors, which are useful for the promotion and circulation of cultural products and are transversal to any cultural sectors.*
STRONGLY CULTURAL SECTORS	**HYBRID-CULTURAL SECTORS**	**FUNCTIONALLY CULTURAL SECTORS**
performing arts, visual arts, cultural heritage, books and press, music, radio, film, television, DVD, video, video games, new media	*a) architecture, design, fashion, advertising b)sport, recreation and tourism*	*intangible cultural heritage, archiving and preserving, education and training, equipment and supporting materials*

can also encompass products linked to culture, since they are aimed at achieving recreation and entertainment functions (i.e., *sport*, *recreation* and *tourism*).

The third dimension is characterized by *functionally cultural sectors*, peculiar of products useful for the production and the distribution of cultural products. In this perspective, they are cross-sector products (defined as *intangible cultural heritage*, *archiving* and *preserving*, *education* and *training*, *equipment* and *supporting materials*).

The perimeter of the audiovisual industry

It is quite easy to notice how each classification can include the audiovisual sectors among cultural ones. However, due to the heterogeneity of audiovisual products, it is difficult to understand whether audiovisual sectors have to be enclosed in strongly cultural sectors or in hybrid ones.

DOI: 10.1057/9781137378477.0008

Indeed, audiovisual products can be related to creativity and intellectual property; meanwhile, they do not have any primary instrumental function. However, not all of them can be recognized as the result of an original creativity, or as characterized by unicity, and, therefore, not all of them can be considered cultural products. This creates a certain discrimination among audiovisual products. Often it concerns the type of products: a film, for example, is usually perceived as a creative product, while TV news is not. Furthermore, with reference to the audiovisual industry, the possibility to reproduce an audiovisual work does not exclude its creative nature: a film is an original creative product, even if it can be reproduced in a variety of copies and in many formats – for example DVDs – aimed at achieving a wider distribution of works. The serial nature of the production process, on the contrary, more than the possibility to reproduce the product, can damage the creative element of audiovisual works. In this perspective, a thousand-episode TV series can certainly suffer from a corruption of its creative aspects more than a single film work.

The need for a working definition of cultural sectors has persuaded policy makers to adopt a more pragmatic approach: the theoretical taxonomy of cultural sectors has been translated into a statistical definition, which also considers international accounting standards for industrial sectors.

The *European Competitiveness Report* by the European Commission can offer more insights about this topic[7]. Moreover, adopting the same approach of the aforementioned KEA study of 2006, as well as UNESCO study of 2009, it defines creative and cultural sectors, suggesting a definition of the perimeter of cultural industry in accordance to NACE classification[8].

The European context assumes significance in the work of the *European Statistical Systems* (ESSnet-Culture), a network of several European Statistical Systems set up at Eurostat in 2009. The study has led to the publication of several guidelines for member States in order to support data collection on culture (ESSnet 2012). The ESSnet-Culture does not only provide a set of cultural domains, but suggests also a link between groups of activities and the NACE codes. The classification of cultural sectors is based upon ten main domains and the corresponding NACE classes and codes[9] (Table 3.3).

NACE section N and P are transversal to all domains, while each single domain includes activities encompassed in one or another of the

DOI: 10.1057/9781137378477.0008

TABLE 3.3 *ESSnet cultural domains and NACE sections*

	NACE CLASSIFICATION					
	Section G	Section J	Section M	Section N	Section P	Section R
ESSnet CULTURAL DOMAINS	Wholesale and Retail Trade	Information and Communications	Professional, Scientific and Technical Activities	Administrative and Support Activities	Education	Arts, Entertainment and Recreation
Heritage				*	*	x
Archives				*	*	x
Libraries				*	*	x
Book & Press	x	x	x	*	*	x
Visual Arts			x	*	*	x
Performing Arts				*	*	x
Audiovisual and Multimedia	x	x		*	*	x
Architecture			x	*	*	
Advertising			x	*	*	
Arts Crafts				*	*	x

DOI: 10.1057/9781137378477.0008

residual NACE codes. It is evident that the audiovisual sector appears to be equally rich, showing activities comprised in different NACE codes. More specifically, the audiovisual sectors are composed of ten sub-sectors identifying different activities and corresponding to specific NACE sections and codes (Table 3.4).

The EU *Audiovisual Media Services Directive* is largely consistent with the ESSnet classification[10]. With reference to an audiovisual media service, The Directive states that "the principal purpose [...] is the provision of programmes, in order to inform, entertain or educate, to the general public" where programmes stands for "a set of moving images with or without sound constituting an individual item within a schedule or a catalogue established by a media service provider and the form and content of which are comparable to the form and content of television broadcasting". Therefore, the Directive regulatory framework concerns products containing moving images, regardless of the content and the aim of the product – information, education, entertainment, commercial communication, advertising. The EU approach is largely consistent with the ESSnet and NACE classification: music, radio and other types of artistic creation are excluded, defining a perimeter of interest roughly corresponding to NACE section J. Besides, the fact that the EU Directive is mainly aimed at regulating TV broadcasters' activities does not imply

TABLE 3.4 *ESSnet delineation of audiovisual activities in NACE sections and codes*

	Audiovisual and Multimedia	
NACE Activities	**NACE Codes**	**NACE Section**
Retail sale of music and video recordings in specialized stores	47.63	G
Publishing of computer games	58.21	J
Motion picture, video and television programme production	59.11	J
Motion picture, video and television programme post-production	59.12	J
Motion picture, video and television programme distribution	59.13	J
Motion picture projection activities	59.14	J
Radio broadcasting	60.10	J
Television programming and broadcasting activities	60.20	J
Renting of video tapes and disks (50%)	77.22	N
Artistic creation	90.03	R

DOI: 10.1057/9781137378477.0008

that similar products produced, provided and broadcasted by actors other than TV firms do not belong to the cluster of audiovisual products, as in the case of films for theatrical release or web products released by new media players.

> Combining the theoretical approaches present in literature with the working definition based upon accounting and statistical classifications, as well as the existing regulatory framework, it is finally possible to state that the audiovisual industry is represented by those industrial sectors characterized by products containing moving images. The nature of the producer, the scope and feature of the products, as well as the way products can be broadcasted and distributed, identifies different audiovisual markets/sectors, each one with its specific regulations, or even non-regulated, as for new emerging ones.

Taking as perspective the distribution model, it is possible to categorize three main audiovisual markets: TV, cinema and web market (Table 3.5). The methodological approach followed in this text is consistent with this last classification.

3.3 The audiovisual products

Based on the distribution model, it is possible to identify TV products, film works and products intended for web distribution. It is worth clarifying that this difference is less relevant than it previously was. Indeed, the evolution of the market has encouraged the distribution of hybrid products. The context of the modern audiovisual market does not facilitate the identification of the primary distribution channel for each product. There is a growing trend to produce, for a single product, a variety of specific adaptations – i.e. remakes, sequels, prequels and spin-offs – for different types of distribution markets. Furthermore, the market is experiencing hybrid products which, since the first creative moment, are designed in order to be placed on different distribution platforms, without requiring any special adaptations. Moreover, new media players – mainly the Over the Top[11] – are starting to produce their own original products, including TV shows and films, that are released via web. The taxonomy hereby presented should also be analysed considering its "work in progress" nature. The possibility to recognize a specific distribution model for every product has to be considered within a perspective based upon convergence and integration.

DOI: 10.1057/9781137378477.0008

TABLE 3.5 *The perimeter of the audiovisual industry*

MARKETS	KIND OF MOVING IMAGES PRODUCTS	STRONG CULTURALITY	HYBRID CULTURALITY	FUNCTIONAL CULTURALITY	REGULATED	NON-REGULATED
TV	information, education, entertainment, communication, advertising	X	X		X	
CINEMA	entertainment	X	X		X	
WEB	information, education, entertainment, communication, advertising	X	X			X

DOI: 10.1057/9781137378477.0008

TV products

If an audiovisual product is designed in order to be exclusively or primarily broadcast, it can be defined as a TV product. According to this approach, it is easy to understand that TV broadcasters do not only schedule TV programmes. This is even more evident if we consider all film works televised after their screening period. TV products, in a general conception, can be imagined as a cluster of audiovisual products that the public can watch on a TV platform, hence being a complex construct. To simplify, it is possible to identify two types of TV products: non-fictional audiovisual works and fiction products (Figure 3.1).

The first cluster is destined to be exclusively shown on TV, while the second can be watched also in other contexts; therefore, television may not be the priority market of exploitation.

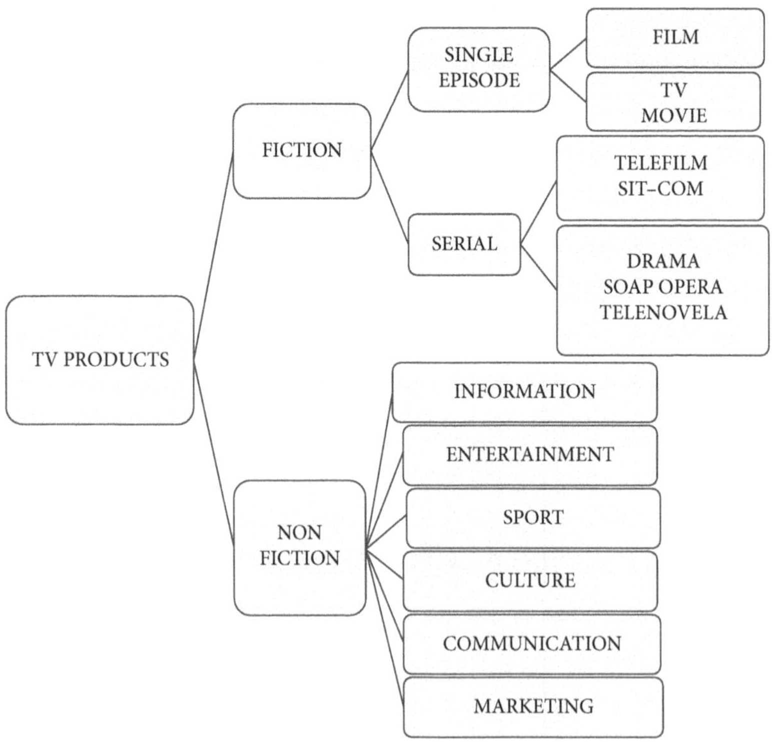

FIGURE 3.1 *Typologies of TV products*

DOI: 10.1057/9781137378477.0008

Fiction products include programmes with a narrative structure and can be created using TV techniques (TV cameras), or cinematographic ones (film cameras).

In particular, fiction products can be divided based on the following points:

- *Single episode products*: include films and TV movies. The first ones are intended to be screened in cinemas, and can be televised only after the theatrical release. TV movies can only be watched on TV.
- *Serial products*, composed of a series of episodes, which have a continuous narration and stable characters; serial products are always designed to be shown on TV. There are many types of serial products:
- *telefilms and situation comedies* (sit-coms), in which characters are stable, but each episode has a different plot;
- *drama, soap operas and telenovelas*, with constant narration and stable characters.

Non fictional programmes include different categories, such as news, entertainment, sport and culture programmes, as well as communication and advertising. Those programmes can be broadcasted live or recorded, while fiction products are always recorded.

Cinema products

Film works are primarily intended to have a theatrical release and are normally sorted by duration or content. Based on the duration in minutes, they can be defined as *feature* or *short films*. They can also be defined as *fiction products* or *documentaries* depending on the presence of specific narrative elements (Figure 3.2).

Fiction products for cinema can be also sorted by genre, that is, by type of content and narrative style. There are many taxonomies for the genres, with different levels of detail. Table 3.6 shows a classification commonly received in USA, in line with the main international classifications.

Often, genre typologies also imply specific subsectors for each genre identified, and they can reach specific descriptive levels. It is interesting to point out that documentaries are considered as a specific type of product, which can also identify a specific editorial genre.

Of course, genre classification, created and used mainly to categorize film works, can be extended to fiction TV products.

DOI: 10.1057/9781137378477.0008

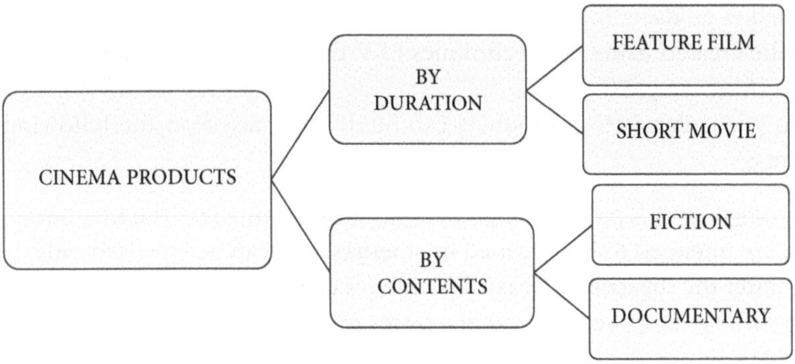

FIGURE 3.2 *Typologies of cinema products*

TABLE 3.6 *The most common genres of films*

GENRES
Action
Adventure
Animation
Comedy
Crime
Documentary
Drama
Family
Fantasy
Horror
Musical
Mystery
Noir
Romance
Sci-Fi or Science Fiction
Short
Thriller
War
Western

The traditional difference between fiction TV products and film works is not explained based on genre, but on the different types of narration styles, duration or the tools used for the shootings: film cameras for films, TV cameras for TV products. However, currently, the differences linked to the type of cameras used are less relevant, due to an increase in the use of digital TV cameras also for film shootings. Simultaneously,

DOI: 10.1057/9781137378477.0008

differences among narrative styles appear to decrease, while duration differences are still relevant.

Web audiovisual products

The web is becoming one of the most powerful distribution tools for audiovisual products. Yet to be completely regulated, the on-line distribution mechanism allows young independent filmmakers to widely spread their works freely to the public. Also due to the mentioned features, products designed for an exclusive or a primary distribution on the web have exponentially increased during the last years. Normally, they are low-budget products, filmed with TV cameras and with poor financial resources. Recently, the most successful media players – mainly the OTT – have entered the market producing their own products[12]. OTT have experienced a great success in offering SVoD services to their customers and have seen their revenues grow over the years; this has enabled them to dispose of a large amount of resources to devote to production. Having their own content allows OTT to be independent of traditional broadcasters, and in particular of the Pay TV which in Europe are the largest holders of the rights of exploitation of films. Unlike young filmmakers, OTT can produce high-budget web products that, in the near future, will coexist and compete with those low-budget products.

Regardless of budget, audiovisual web products, typically, have a short duration, often, but not always, few number of episodes. The creative freedom of the web has encouraged the increase in the number of product types, many of them not to be categorized based on traditional standards. The advantageous use of a categorization is based upon a first difference between fiction and non-fictional products (Figure 3.3).

Web products, such as fiction works, cannot be sorted by genre, in particular not by cinematographic traditional genres. On the contrary, they can be categorized based on their specific format: therefore, web series represent the main innovative element. Web series have a very short duration – 30 seconds to 25 minutes – with an average duration of 7 minutes per episode. Web series are now very popular; in particular, they are followed both by young and adult people, due to their creative spontaneity, as well as an easy way to access the contents, because of the short duration[13]. Since web platforms assure a viral diffusion of the series, they foster users to share their emotional experience with other

DOI: 10.1057/9781137378477.0008

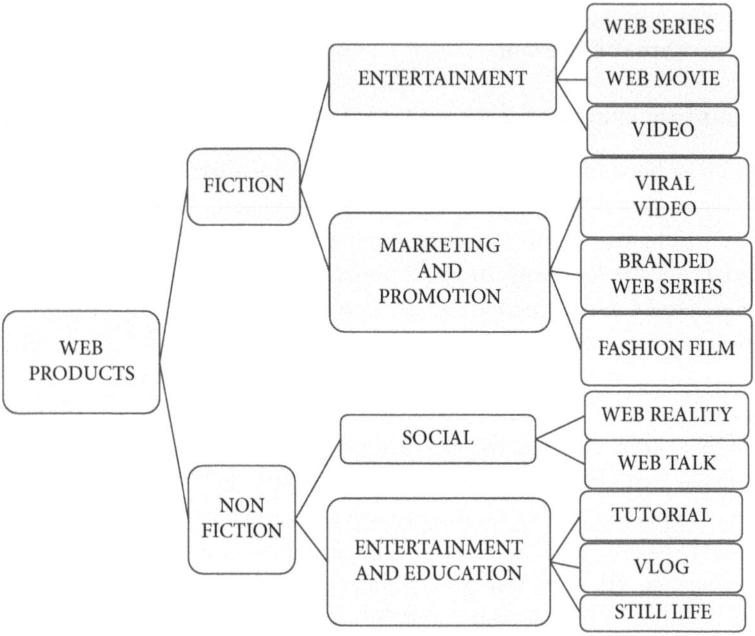

FIGURE 3.3 *Typologies of web audiovisual products*

unknown users, or members of specific communities. Among web series, comedy sketches, comedy stories, drama, horror, fiction, fantasy, mockumentaries, as well as documentaries and musicals are the most common genres.

Due to their peculiarities and for the immediate feedback possible to get from the public, nowadays web series are beginning to have a certain relevance for traditional TV and film production companies, especially for their talent scout activity. This explains why many festivals dedicated to web series have been springing up in recent years, while film festivals are beginning to include special sessions for these products[14].

The capability to assure great levels of viral circulation to successful products, has encouraged the development of two types of peculiar web products: those using web as a marketing and promotion tool, and those based upon social features of web products, quite similar to many typical TV formats.

With reference to the first type, it is possible to identify three kinds of specific fiction products: viral videos, branded web series and fashion

DOI: 10.1057/9781137378477.0008

films. The first type is a non-serial product, with a very short duration – usually a few seconds or a few moments, a narrative content aimed at sensitizing people on social, custom, environmental or economic topics, or at promoting brands or products. Branded web series are serial products with a narrative feature, focussed on the circulation of a specific brand, as well as the style of a particular company. Fashion films are non-serial products, created with the specific purpose of promoting popular brands, and do not necessarily have to include a narrative element.

With reference to the second type, other kinds of products, similar to non-fictional TV programmes, can be included. In particular, web realities and web talks are very popular. Peculiar of web products are also many audiovisual works that can be include in a specific cluster half-way between education and entertainment: those products known as "tutorials", vlogs and still life videos. The first videos are aimed at teaching specific activities, the second ones correspond to a video version of blogs – in this case protagonists are defined and known as "YouTubers". Still life videos are moving pictures related to specific topics with a variety of contents and an almost completely emotional message.

Notes

1 For a review of the literature, see O'Brien 2010.
2 See Holden 2006.
3 See Throsby 2001.
4 KEA 2006.
5 European Commission 2010a.
6 UNESCO 2009.
7 European Commission 2010b.
8 NACE (in French: "nomenclature statistique des activités économiques dans la Communauté européenne") is a European industry standard classification system consisting of a six-digit code. The 2010 European Competitiveness Report used the NACE rev.2.
9 The ESSnet used the NACE rev.2.
10 EU Directive 2010/13.
11 The so called Over the Top are those pure Internet players offering subscription video on demand (SVoD) services. For more details on OTT: European Audiovisual Observatory (2014).
12 The first OTT to invest in original contents was Netflix with *Lilyhammer*, *Arrested Development* and *House of Cards*.

DOI: 10.1057/9781137378477.0008

13 For more details on web series market, see: Gangemi et al. (2013)
14 Among the most famous festivals dedicated to web series: Austin, Carballo Inter Play, DC Web Fest, Los Angeles Web Series Festival, Marseille Web Fest, Miami Web Fest, Melbourne Web Fest, Roma Web Fest, Toronto Web Fest and Vancouver Web Fest.

DOI: 10.1057/9781137378477.0008

OPEN

4 Costs and Revenues of Audiovisual Products

Abstract: *The analysis of the costs and revenues concerning audiovisual products is the starting point of any theory of value and is instrumental to the understanding of pricing and financial dynamics of the audiovisual industry and single companies. In this chapter different types of costs related to the production and distribution of audiovisual products, as well as possible revenue sources, are analysed, distinguishing between TV products, films and audiovisual web products. The chapter is not intended to be a mere classification of costs, nor a handbook on the costs and revenues measures. It is rather an attempt to build a methodology to analyse the economics of the audiovisual industry.*

La Torre, Mario. *The Economics of the Audiovisual Industry: Financing TV, Film and Web.* Basingstoke: Palgrave Macmillan, 2014. DOI: 10.1057/9781137378477.0009.

4.1 Introduction

In market practice, the value of an audiovisual product can be expressed both as a cost, when referring to the production stage, and as a price, when referring to the negotiation stage. The analysis of the costs and revenues concerning audiovisual products is the starting point of any theory of value and is instrumental to the understanding of pricing and financial dynamics of the audiovisual industry and single companies. In this chapter different types of costs related to the production and distribution of audiovisual products, as well as possible revenue sources, are analysed distinguishing between TV products, films and audiovisual web products. The chapter is not intended to be a mere classification of costs, nor a handbook on the costs and revenues measures. It is rather an attempt to build a methodology to analyse the economics of the audiovisual industry.

4.2 Typologies of costs and sources of revenues

The overall cost of an audiovisual product may be divided into different types of spending. It is possible to distinguish five categories of costs: (a) pre-production costs related to the development of the project, (b) artistic production costs, (c) technical production costs, (d) post-production costs and (e) distribution costs (Figure 4.1 and Table 4.1).

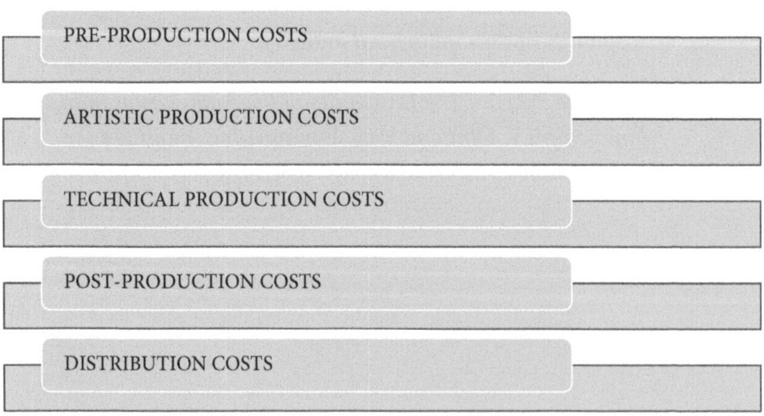

FIGURE 4.1 *Typologies of costs of audiovisual products*

DOI: 10.1057/9781137378477.0009

TABLE 4.1 *The costs of audiovisual products*

TYPOLOGIES OF COSTS	COST ITEMS
PRE-PRODUCTION COSTS	Storyline and Screenplay Preparation: Project Research and Development Feasibility Study Pre-recruitment of Technical and Artistic Resources
ARTISTIC PRODUCTION COSTS	Director Cast
TECHNICAL PRODUCTION COSTS	Producer Fee Editing Crew Extra Talent Wardrobe Set Location Transportation Music Publicity Fringes Insurance Equipment
POST-PRODUCTION COSTS	Post-production Film & Lab Editing

The pre-production costs are attributable to the creative idea at the very core of an audiovisual project, to the feasibility study of the project, to its development up to the first supply of technical and artistic resources necessary for the production. The cost of the creative idea is represented mainly by the cost of so-called "plot or storyline" and the subsequent screenplay.

The storyline and screenplay can be original and created *ad hoc*, original but already existing, or non-original and derived from literary works – in the last two cases the cost coincides with the purchase price of the plot rights, the screenplay rights, or the rights to the literary work.

Production costs are divided into artistic costs – generally referred to the director and main actors – and technical costs that include all the costs related to the crew engaged in the production, location costs, set and wardrobe, as well as the costs of advertising and promotion.

Post-production costs comprise all costs related to the editing of the film, in particular images and sound editing, and special effects.

DOI: 10.1057/9781137378477.0009

Distribution costs relate to both the costs of accessing a specific distribution platform through which the public may watch the product and the costs of communication and marketing.

> The extent of individual cost items, and its significance as the percentage of the overall budget are strongly dependent on the product typology. Audiovisual products, despite being subject to the same manufacturing process, are the result of a mix of artistic and technical elements that will differ for different types of products. Moreover, strategic choices may have an impact on the nature of production costs and their extent.

The analysis of costs, therefore, should be conducted with reference to the type of product and to the priority distribution channel.

When analysing the revenues, it is important to clarify how audiovisual products fall into the category of "experience goods", from an economic point of view, and in that of "intangible assets", from an accounting point of view. In other words, audiovisual products are goods expressing an intangible value related to the emotional satisfaction of the audience and, for this reason, are classified as "experiential goods". This explains why the capacity of an audiovisual product to generate revenues depends directly on the will of the public to pay for the possibility to watch the product, and thus transforms itself from potential audience to actual viewers. The more actual-paying viewers an audiovisual product attracts, the more revenues it generates. Therefore, the revenues are related to the product's capacity to attract paying viewers on various markets of exploitation.

> The nature and volume of revenues generated by an audiovisual product are linked to the economic exploitation of the product, and the product, in turn, is linked to the channels used by the public to watch it. Exploitation rights for an audiovisual product refer to the right of economic exploitation of the same.

Therefore, exploitation rights may not coincide with the ownership of the work, but still they entitle their holder to economic exploitation of the product, meaning the possibility to obtain revenues from its sale or from licensing the right to it.

The main forms of economic exploitation coincide with the main and most widespread forms of watching audiovisual products: cinema, television, home video and the web. The access to different markets of exploitation is linked to different market practices and regulatory constraints that define a precise timing of usability of the audiovisual

DOI: 10.1057/9781137378477.0009

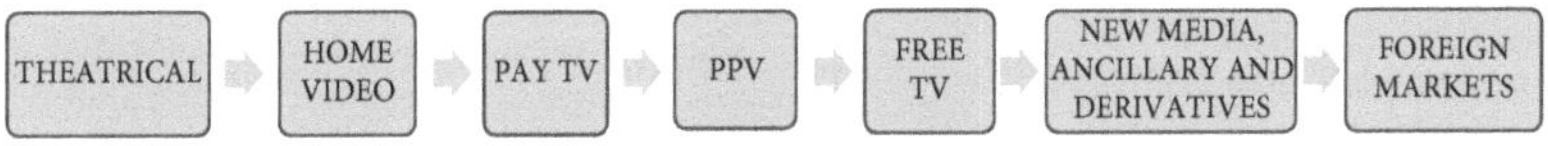

FIGURE 4.2 *Windows of exploitation*

product through various forms of exploitation: the time slots dedicated to different exploitation markets are called "windows" (Figure 4.2). In an international context, the windows have different durations but the chronological sequence of exploitation is sufficiently harmonized and, for a product which can access all forms of exploitation, mainly cinema works, the first window is the movie theatre, followed by Home Video (HD), Pay TV, PPV, Free TV, and other ancillary and derivatives markets, including the ones related to new technologies: new Media and Video on demand (the so called "VOD"). These new technological markets allow a non-linear and interactive use of a work. The most important among ancillary markets are merchandising, advertising (the use of images or sequences of images to promote products), sponsorship (the use of images or their sequences linked to the sponsor's name), premium promotion (use of promotional items relating to characters distributed freely for promotional purposes regarding products or services) and recording (separate use of the work and the soundtrack). The most important among derivative markets are those exploiting the rights for sequel, prequel, remake, spin-off (a work derived from an already existing work that focuses on one of the characters and develops a whole new plot) and novelization (adaptation of a story from another medium).

Foreign market is a specific source of potential revenue regarding the possibility of selling the rights to exploit a work in a country other than that in which it was produced, and so it is independent from the timing of other windows of exploitation.

The new tendencies in the audiovisual market, and the subsequent creation of hybrid cross media products, result in the traditional linear pattern of windows of exploitation becoming less representative. The access timing to the windows is becoming more and more irregular and there is an increasing number of products which are meant for one specific window only (Figure 4.3).

Technical and artistic characteristics of a product determine also its potential access to exploitation markets. Different products will have different capacities to generate revenues, also with reference to different exploitation markets (Figure 4.4).

DOI: 10.1057/9781137378477.0009

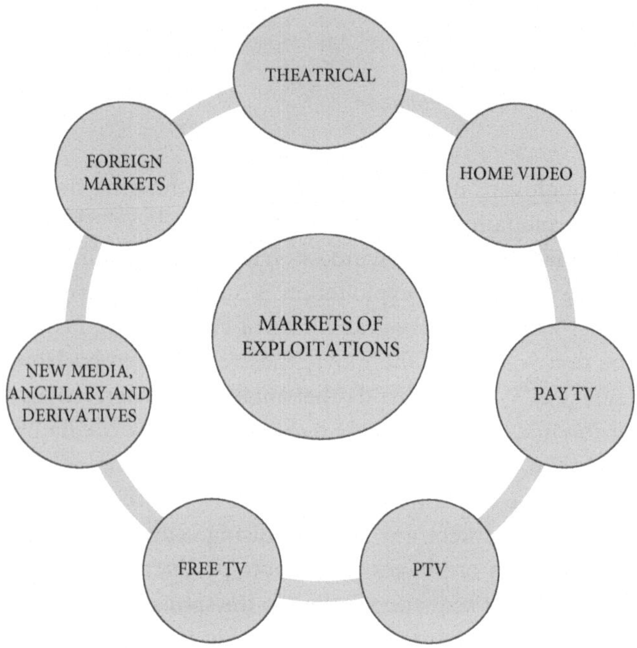

FIGURE 4.3 *Markets of exploitations*

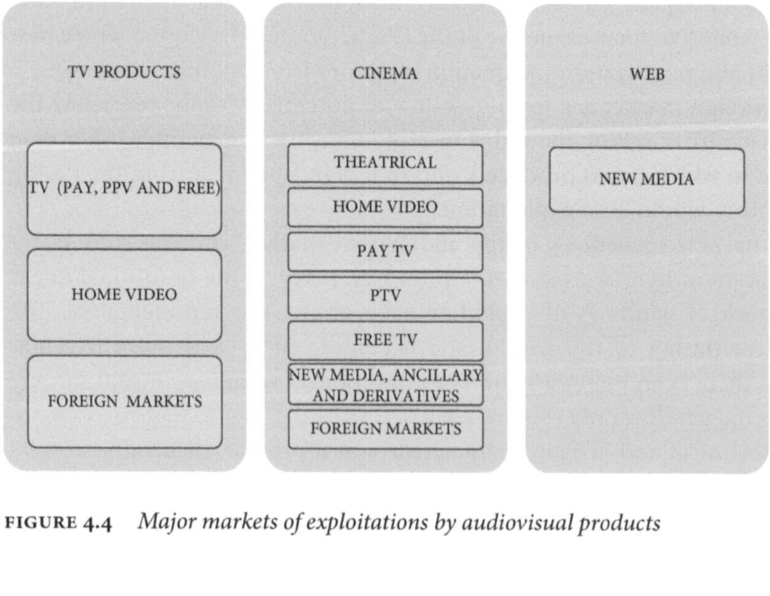

FIGURE 4.4 *Major markets of exploitations by audiovisual products*

DOI: 10.1057/9781137378477.0009

As a matter of fact, film products may be classified as products with a longer cycle of exploitation, as they are potentially able to access all forms of exploitation. The audience may watch a film both in the cinema and on TV, as well as in Home Video mode or through modern technologies on new channels based on Internet connection. On the contrary, TV and web products are usually characterized by a limited number of exploitation channels, even if the new generation of cross media products is going to picture a different landscape for the next future. The possibility of accessing a foreign market, and its significance in terms of percentage in the revenues in relation to the overall revenue generated by a work, is a peculiar characteristic of only a few products. Products' internationality depends on various factors: artistic qualities of the product, including both the universality of the story and the popularity of the cast and director.

Finally, it should also be clarified why a major number of potential exploitation channels does not necessarily coincide with major economic potential. And it is due to the fact that some exploitation channels are more profitable than others. On the other hand, however, there are also those forms of exploitation that do not generate any revenue at all.

In the light of the above mentioned, the analysis of costs and revenues generated by an audiovisual product should be conducted by examining some of the peculiarities distinguishing television, cinema and web products.

4.3 Costs and revenues of TV products

Costs of TV products

There is a clear correlation between the typology of a TV product, its artistic quality, its production model and the nature and extent of costs it generates (Figure 4.5).

When considering the typology of a product in relation to the costs and their significance, the most visible differences emerge between

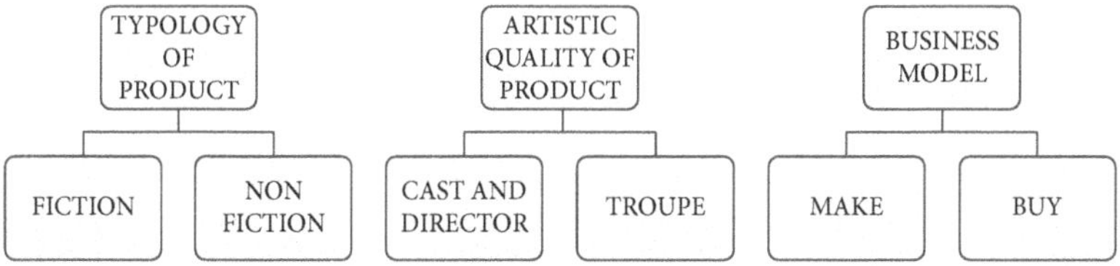

FIGURE 4.5 *Determinants of costs for TV products*

DOI: 10.1057/9781137378477.0009

fiction and non-fiction. While the costs of fiction products are generated throughout the entire production process (pre-production, artistic and technical production, post-production), for non-fiction products the pre- and post-production costs are much less significant.

In general terms, low pre-production costs are a result of the absence of the creative element in non-fiction productions. Also, non-fictional programmes are usually broadcasted live, which significantly reduces the post-production costs. However, there are cases in which non-fiction productions do generate significant pre-production costs and it usually happens with productions based on formats purchased from third parties – the purchase of exploitation rights being the main component of pre-production costs.

The relative significance of individual cost items, on the other hand, rather than being a function of the nature of TV product, is usually a function of the quality standard of the product, and often is strongly dependent on the artistic and technical crew engaged in the production. Therefore, it can be affirmed that the cost items that have the greatest impact on the production budget are artistic and technical production costs. Naturally, the value of these cost items, and their percentage in the total budget, depend mainly on the artistic element and not on the type of programme. Engaging well-known and acclaimed directors and actors increases the budget of fiction productions. But there are also examples of news that generate higher costs when compared to entertainment shows only because an influential journalist is involved.

The cost of a programme is also related to the production model adopted by a television company. In order to satisfy the need for new programmes, a TV company may either make them or buy them and, therefore, decide on one of the following:

a. *in-house production*: the TV company produces and finances the production;
b. *co-production*: the TV company participates in the production and covers only a part of the total production costs;
c. *commissioned production*: the production is contracted to third-party independent executive producers, but financed by the TV company;
d. *purchase*: the TV company purchases programmes from other producers/broadcasters.

The above-mentioned alternatives differ in terms of the nature of production costs and their extent (Figure 4.6). In the case of in-house production or co-production, the television company will directly incur

DOI: 10.1057/9781137378477.0009

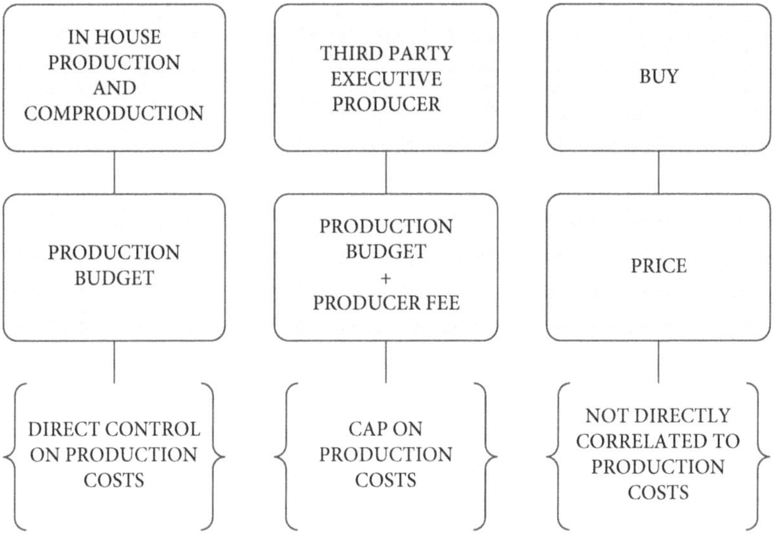

FIGURE 4.6 *Costs and business models for TV products*

the total production cost or its share in the production costs. In the case of a production commissioned to an executive producer, the costs are always covered by the TV company (the contractor), including a fee for the executive producer (the contracting). These two options differ in terms of a degree of control that the TV company has over the production costs: direct and independent control in the first option; indirect control dependent on the ability of the executive producer in the latter one. TV companies usually establish a cap on production costs that the third party producer needs to observe and any additional costs are covered by the executive producer – which means that the costs incurred by the commissioning company do not change.

When purchasing a programme, the product cost is the purchasing price, which may be uncorrelated to the production costs. The determinants of prices and costs for TV products represent key factors in the theory of value of audiovisual products and are the fundamental variables in explaining the pricing of these products[1].

At this point, it is necessary to explain why the choice of a business model for TV products is primarily based on variables of editorial and strategic nature, rather than on economic ones. From the editorial

DOI: 10.1057/9781137378477.0009

point of view an in-house production is always the first choice for those programmes that are supposed to be easily associated with the company's brand, or if the company wants to maintain a direct control over its content. Therefore, for editorial reasons, in-house production involves usually non-fictional programmes, customarily news. Such an approach is justified also by some strategic variables. A decision to outsource production is a medium- to long-term strategic choice because it has an impact on the entire company's structure and on its balance sheet.

It should be noted that purchase costs (*buy* alternative) are usually bigger but more flexible whereas production costs (*make* alternative) are significantly more rigid. Producing in house, rather than commissioning or purchasing, means developing structures and skills which will probably lead to a substantial increase in overhead expense.

The need to brand news and information programmes and to assure availability of the product when needed for programming is not so urgent in the case of fiction products. When it comes to fiction, the decision whether to make or to buy is strictly based on economic variables, and the cost-benefits analysis involves the following factors:

a) the extent and rigidity of the fixed costs related to the in-house production;
b) the purchase price, including all kinds of fees due to any third parties and intermediaries.

If the demand for a given product declines, the *buy* alternative allows greater flexibility to change one's mind and take a different course of action. Deciding on the *make* alternative can be justified only in case of information products and news – strongly linked to the brand – and in case of those fiction products that ensure significant production volumes and long-term audience loyalty.

For these reasons, the main television broadcasters (including the four national television networks in the USA: ABC, NBC, CBC, Fox) produce only a limited number of programmes in-house, commissioning the production of fiction to film companies, and the production of entertainment shows to audiovisual production companies.

Finally, even if the *make* alternative results more convenient in terms of costs-benefits analysis, one should also consider the financial sustainability of the choice. The investment needed for in-house production may be unsustainable for the company, as it may require too high initial investment with revenues diluted over time. This element is of fundamental

DOI: 10.1057/9781137378477.0009

importance for the understanding of the coherence of the purchase price of an audiovisual product, and it also explains why the purchasing price is usually high. And therefore, even if the cost of in-house production results lower when compared with the purchase cost, the company may still decide on *buy* alternative keeping in mind the strategic flexibility it guarantees in case of any change in market trends. Higher costs incurred in time *t* would thus be compensated by minor costs of changing strategy in time *t+1*. In the medium-term, the cost-benefit analysis may lead to the conclusion that the *buy* alternative is cheaper. In the medium- to long-term, it may be more convenient to opt for the purchase even at costs higher than those of an in-house production. Such a perspective may lead a TV company to accept high purchase prices, even those exceeding significantly the costs of in-house production.

In general terms, it can be observed that: (a) television companies decide on in-house production when it comes to news and information programmes; (b) the most frequently chosen business models for entertainment programmes are commissioned production and in-house production; (c) commissioning, co-production and purchase are alternatives mostly applied to fiction.

In conclusion, it can be stated that (Figure 4.7):

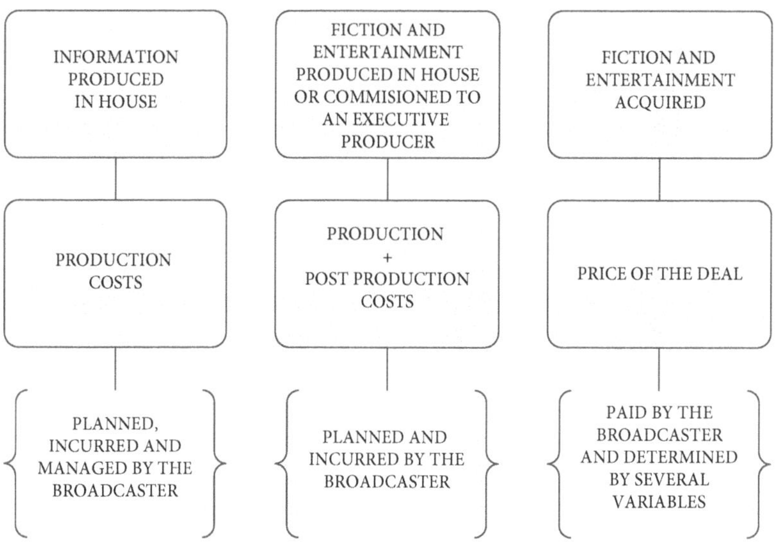

FIGURE 4.7 *Costs of TV products by typology and business models*

DOI: 10.1057/9781137378477.0009

a) news and information programmes are usually made in-house and broadcasted live – the costs are incurred directly by the television company and refer mainly to the production stage;
b) fiction and entertainment programmes can be produced in-house or commissioned – the costs are incurred directly by the television company and refer to all production stages;
c) fiction and entertainment products can be acquired – the cost is the purchase price and its determinants are diverse and different, depending on the product and on the territory, and are conditioned by historical periods and economic cycles.

Revenues of TV products

The natural media outlet for television products is television itself. Recently, certain television products falling into the fiction category can also be found in Home Video and other markets, mainly VOD.

With reference to in-house production, co-production and commissioned production, the original owner of exploitation rights is the television broadcaster. In the case of purchase, the television company acquires the right of exploitation from the original producer or from a third party who owns such rights.

Broadcasting revenues, regardless of whether the product has been acquired or produced in-house, consist mostly of advertising revenues attributable to that product. Advertising revenues depend not only on the typology of the product but also on its capacity to attract audience, as well as its position in programme schedule and, therefore, on its time slot and the channel on which it is aired. These are the variables taken into consideration by the advertisers when deciding on airing their commercials within a given programme and on charge rates they are willing to pay for it[2].

For the producer, or a third party owner of exploitation rights, television revenue is embodied in the sale price of the exploitation right to a broadcaster who intends to air the programme. The price is influenced by the potential advertising revenue associated with the product.

In brief, it is possible to state that the revenues deriving from television exploitation rights of an audiovisual product are directly and indirectly linked to the advertising revenues that a broadcaster is able to obtain from the product. It is not possible to draw a clear distinction between products of fiction and non-fiction when it comes to their capacity of

DOI: 10.1057/9781137378477.0009

generating revenues. Advertisers assess attractiveness of a given product by analysing both historic and estimated audience data. With the exception of certain specific events – such as national or international sporting championships – there are no rules that would explain why some programmes are more attractive than others. Some types of audiovisual products primarily destined for television exploitation are fortunate to penetrate also other markets, like Home Video, VOD or foreign markets. However, with very few exceptions, these forms of exploitations are decidedly of a marginal significance in terms of revenues.

Finally, it might be useful to explain how the governance model of the television broadcaster affects sales of individual products (Figure 4.8). Revenues of a public television broadcaster derive not only from advertising, but also from Government grants and from local authorities' contributions. Public broadcasters and pay TV also have the advantage of having an additional revenue source that is TV license fees and subscriptions. These additional revenue sources determine different business models and financial cycles of public television, when compared to commercial television, as they do not refer to a single product but to the entire range of products offered by a given television company. In these circumstances it becomes a matter of complicated analysis estimating revenue generated by a single product. On one hand, the methods used by broadcasters to define the portion of the

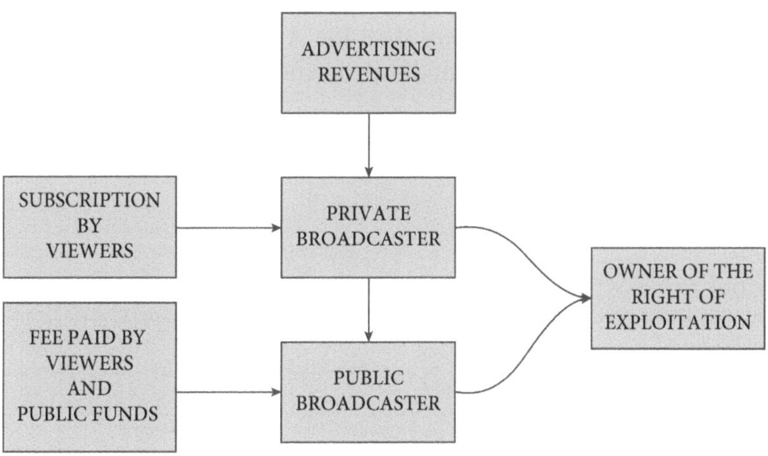

FIGURE 4.8 *Revenues of TV products*

DOI: 10.1057/9781137378477.0009

additional resources attributable to the individual product are influenced by a large margin of discretion; on the other hand, the availability of these resources impacts on the exploitation value of the single product: the price that the broadcaster is willing to pay to buy the product is inevitably affected by the portion of public contribution attributed to the product itself.

4.4 Costs and revenues of cinema products

As for the nature and typology of costs and revenues, it is useful to divide cinema products into traditional fiction productions, animated feature films, documentaries and short films.

Costs of cinema products

The four categories of cinema products involve the same cost typologies as those analysed for television products. There are, however, some differences in terms of individual cost items and their significance as, for example, the distribution costs.

Therefore, costs of cinema products can be classified in two typologies: the costs that are strictly related to production and those related to distribution (Figure 4.9).

Costs of cinema products vary in size and time, depending on the project and on the market: the average production and distribution cost of European films is much lower than the American ones and this is usually explained by the different dimension of the potential revenues of the USA films.

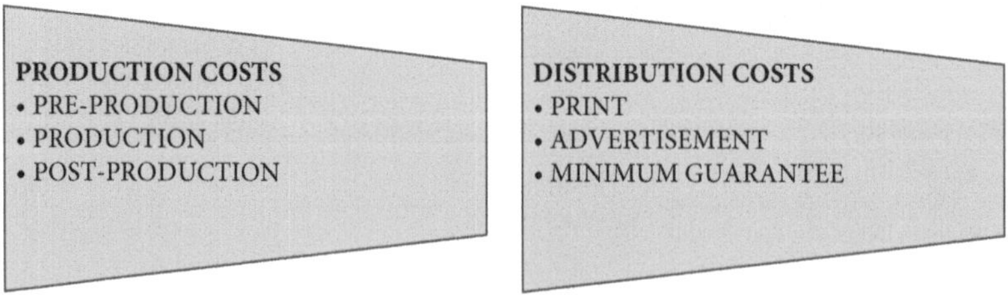

FIGURE 4.9 *Costs of cinema products*

DOI: 10.1057/9781137378477.0009

Production costs: similarly to TV products, production costs can be divided, per time of expenditure, into pre-production, production and post-production, according to time scheduling (Table 4.1).

Average costs of feature films are much higher than those of animated films, documentaries and short films. There are, however, examples of big-budget animated feature films and those of low-budget feature films.

In general terms, it is possible to identify the production costs as the primary outflows regarding a film project. The cost items that weigh heavily on the production budget of feature films include director and cast, artistic and technical crew, and lab costs. In the case of documentaries and animated feature films the absence of costs regarding actors lowers the significance of artistic production costs with an increase in development and post-production costs. Short films, usually produced by young artists taking their first steps in the film industry, reflect in terms of costs, a very low-budget feature film and are often characterized by a productive structure of *amateur* nature that relies strongly on voluntary contributions of the cast and crew and on low-cost services.

Distribution costs of cinema products regard all the activities necessary to access cinemas, as well as all the advertising and promotional activities, which are all part of film distribution. Distribution costs are connected to all the activities aimed at releasing the film on screen in a given territory, such as acquisition of the exploitation rights to the film (so called "minimum guarantee") and the costs incurred by its distributor for the dubbing, as well as for the promotion and launch (Table 4.2).

For feature films and animated films, the cost items that mainly affect the distribution costs are dubbing, printing of copies and advertising (mainly through posters, newspapers and television).

Distribution costs of documentaries and short films are characterized by a different significance and composition, as these two film categories are known to be suffering a constant difficulty in accessing cinema distribution.

Revenues of cinema products

Revenues are linked to the capacity of cinema products to penetrate different markets of exploitation. There are noticeable differences between feature films, animations, documentaries and short movies.

DOI: 10.1057/9781137378477.0009

TABLE 4.2 *Distribution costs of cinema products*

COST TYPOLOGIES	COST ITEMS
DISTRIBUTION RIGHTS	
Acquisition of distribution rights	Minimum guarantee paid by the distributor
EDITING	
Dubbing	Dialogue adaptation/Dubbing
Subtitles	
Censorship	
Printing	Filming/ Trailer
LAUNCH	
Advertising	Posters/Flyers
Press Office	Press book/Photographs/Press Conference
TV/Radio Spot	
Web	
Premieres and Events	
Merchandising	

Feature films are the category characterized by the most complex and varied composition of revenues, owing to their capacity to access different exploitation markets. Virtually, a feature film can access all forms of exploitation existing in various markets. Documentaries are usually screened through television or Home Video; only few feature-length documentaries have the opportunity to access movie theatres. The screening of short films takes place during specialized film festivals or through culturally oriented cinema networks.

Once again, it is important to emphasize how the temporal order of the exploitation windows, characterizing the distribution market of audiovisual products since World War II, is becoming increasingly blurred. A growing number of irregularities has been observed regarding the time and sequence of accessing different markets, as well as time of permanence of a given product on the market. While in the past the access windows outlined a linear distribution process, nowadays the distribution model is rather circular. Access to individual markets has become dependent on the product characteristics, and not on the order of priority established by law or market practices. The modern distribution model, therefore, emphasizes even more the differences between products that were designed and created for specific markets only and universal products. The first group of products finds its access channel only to specific markets, while the second one to the whole distribution

DOI: 10.1057/9781137378477.0009

chain. Both groups access markets in a non-linear manner, but according to distribution strategy and to the audience response (Figure 4.3).

The current trend results in a new blend of the quantitative and qualitative dimension of revenues. In the past, the breakdown of the traditional sources of revenue on the European film market has seen in theatrical the main market of exploitation of rights, followed by Home Video, DVD and television. Since World War II, the characteristic feature of the European film market has been a definite concentration of revenues on specific markets of exploitation. In the United States, by contrast, the market has ensured a greater diversification of revenues and, what is more important, a greater balance between theatrical revenues, Home Video and DVD. Research conducted by IMCA in 2001, on behalf of the European Commission, on a sample of 120 films (108 of European origin and 12 from the USA) revealed that 77% of the total revenue generated by European films derived from theatrical exploitation, 14% from Video and DVD, 3% from Pay TV and 5% from Free TV. In the USA, the situation was completely different – theatrical exploitation generating only 34% of total revenues, Home Video and DVD 41%, Pay TV 17% and Free TV 9%[3]. These results are no longer representative of the current situation that can no longer be described by a rigid revenues composition. Each individual product has a unique range of features that determine their potential penetration of different markets. And the markets themselves are subject to a cyclicality of their profitability.

4.5 Costs and revenues of audiovisual web products

Costs of audiovisual web products

Costs of audiovisual web products reflect the same categories of costs typical of television and cinema products. The production process does not differ in any way, neither in nature, nor in its temporal order. The pre-production, production and post-production costs are a common feature of audiovisual web products as well.

Nevertheless, the nature and the extent of costs are in a way affected by the specific characteristic of web products and of their producer. Here we can distinguish two models. The traditional one is characterized by the circumstance that authors and producers are represented by the same person, or the same group of people. Web products are the

DOI: 10.1057/9781137378477.0009

result of a handyman author who realizes all stages of the production process and, for this reason is commonly called the "filmmaker". Thus, a filmmaker is the person who performs both purely authorial functions, as well as productive and distributive ones. It is common that filmmaking teams are formed essentially on the basis of friendship relationships and shared interests. The control over all production stages allows the filmmakers to measure the costs of a given product and relate them to the available financial means. As filmmakers are usually independent young talents gaining their first professional experience, web products are usually low-budget products. Taking into consideration the nature and the extent of costs, it is possible to make a distinction between artistic production costs, referring to all authors of the product, and technical production costs, which depend on the financial capacities of filmmakers themselves, while distribution costs are reduced almost to zero (Figure 4.10). Web products are exclusively designed for being distributed within the web, while the virality of the web allows for a free marketing campaign.

The costs measure is also strongly affected by the duration of the product. In this perspective, and taking into consideration how vast the range of web audiovisual products is, it is possible to notice significant differences of costs, even between products of the same type, which are due to the product's duration. As an example, a web series can be composed of episodes that may vary from 30 seconds to 20 minutes.

Exceptions to the model described above can be observed in two emerging trends: OTT productions and marketing and communication-

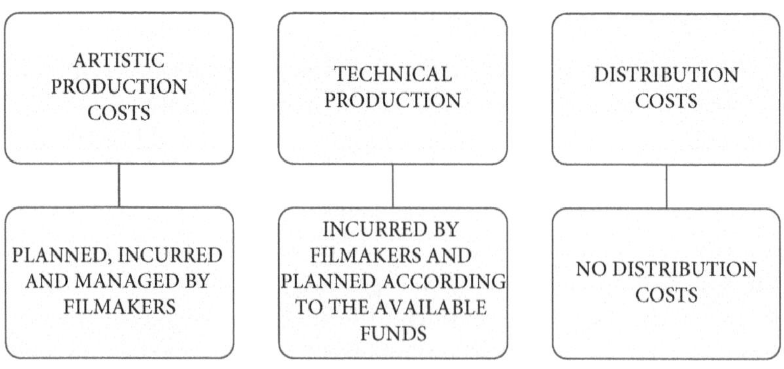

FIGURE 4.10 *Costs of audiovisual web products*

DOI: 10.1057/9781137378477.0009

driven products, such as branded web series and fashion films. These products are promoted and sponsored by OTT to expand their offer of original contents or by a given company in order to promote a brand or a product. In these cases, the filmmakers assume the role of "executive filmmakers" whose task is to simply package the product, conveying a specific message, in a specific editorial style accepted by the promoter-sponsor. The budget of such productions may be significantly higher than average and it depends strongly on the funding coming from the OTT or from the sponsoring company.

Revenues of audiovisual web products

The common feature of native web products is their capacity to generate low revenues when compared to traditional audiovisual products. They are designed for the web and their only distribution channel is the web. At a first stage, potential revenues may be found exclusively in the exploitation of rights on the web platforms. The major revenue source for a web product, as for television products, is the sale of advertising space; when these products are released via SVoD, revenues from subscription fees are also relevant.

Web advertising may take a form of a video or a banner. Different platforms adopt different selling mechanisms for advertising space. It is also common to find different selling mechanism within the same platform. According to this, it is possible to distinguish: advertising-free products, which can be accessed without seeing any advertising messages; semi-free products, with skippable messages like pre-roll, mid-roll or post-roll videos, which can be interrupted by the viewer after few seconds; and restricted-access products, containing an unskippable advertising.

Advertising-free products do note generate any revenues, the revenues from semi-free and restricted-access products depend on agreements between the platform, agents and advertisers, as well as between the platforms and the filmmakers (Figure 4.11). However, the lack of transparency regarding the above-mentioned contractual arrangements hinders proper analysis of the economic dynamics of revenue generation and allocation. In general terms, the central element of agreements with advertisers is the cost per view, according to which the price is correlated to the number of viewers, and, in the case of semi-free products, to the time of permanence of the viewer in the advertising space.

DOI: 10.1057/9781137378477.0009

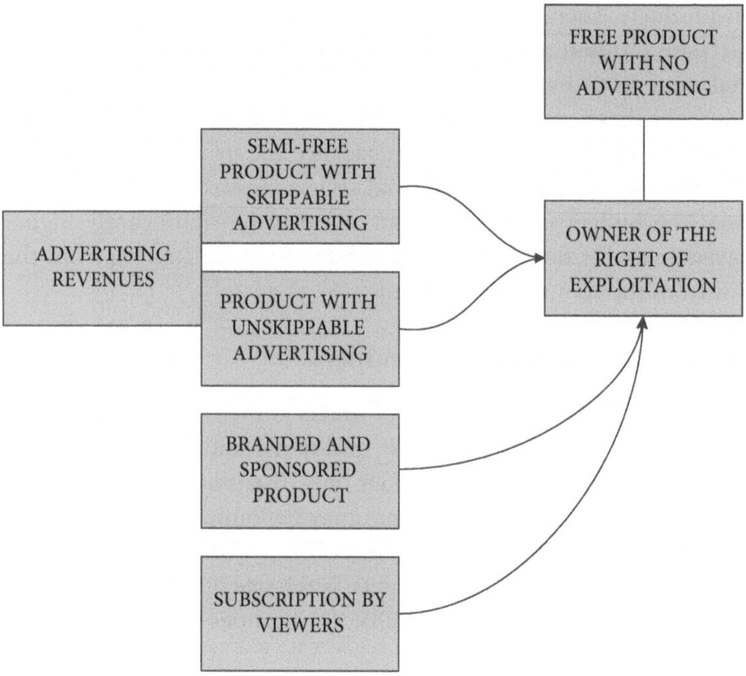

FIGURE 4.11 *Revenues of audiovisual web products*

In the case of sponsored products, as in the case of web series and branded fashion films, the producer fee that the sponsor pays to the filmmaker can be considered as revenue.

Notes

1 Price and value of audiovisual products will be analysed in Chapter 5.
2 For a more detailed analysis of the relationship between the programme schedule and the product's value see Chapter 7.
3 For more details see IMCA (2001) and Adler (2003b).

DOI: 10.1057/9781137378477.0009

OPEN

5
Price and Value of Audiovisual Products

Abstract: *When an audiovisual product is being traded, the costs and revenues related to it are not sufficient to express its value; on the contrary, it is necessary to analyse the dynamics of pricing. Price can be considered a synthetic indicator of the exchange value. However, price is influenced by variables related to the functioning and structure of the market itself. Therefore, while the analysis of costs and revenues represent the basis for the pricing of audiovisual products, it must also be accompanied by the study of two more variables, namely: demand and competition.*

The chapter proposes a theory of pricing and value related to audiovisual products based on classic literature on pricing, suitably contextualised to the audiovisual industry.

La Torre, Mario. *The Economics of the Audiovisual Industry: Financing TV, Film and Web.* Basingstoke: Palgrave Macmillan, 2014. DOI: 10.1057/9781137378477.0010.

5.1 Introduction

When an audiovisual product is being traded, the costs and revenues related to it are not sufficient to express its value; on the contrary it is necessary to analyse the dynamics of pricing. Price can be considered a synthetic indicator of the exchange value. However, since it is functional to the sale of the product on the market, price is influenced by variables related to the functioning and structure of the market itself. Therefore, while the analysis of costs and revenues represents the basis for the pricing of audiovisual products, it must also be accompanied by the study of two more variables, namely: demand and competition.

This chapter proposes a theory of pricing and value related to audiovisual products based on classic literature on pricing, suitably contextualized to the audiovisual industry. The theoretical model is a useful tool for audiovisual companies, financial intermediaries and potential funders of production processes.

5.2 A theoretical framework for pricing

The study of price matches with the analysis of pricing policies which, in turn, define strategies and pricing models related to specific determinants, as well as the price level and structure (Figure 5.1).

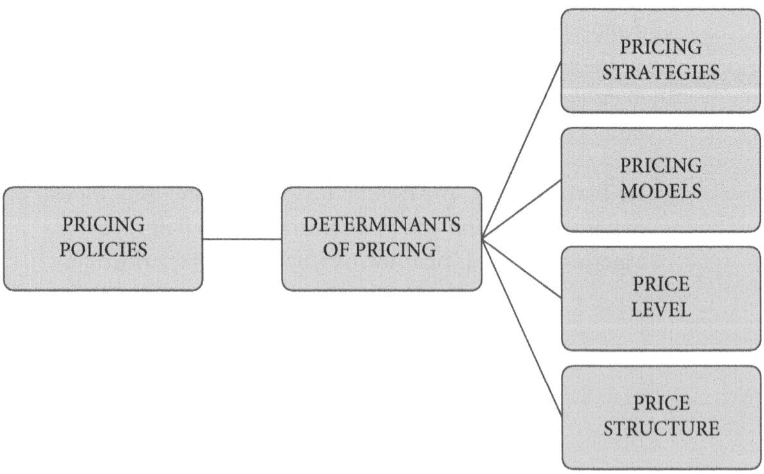

FIGURE 5.1 *Pricing policies*

DOI: 10.1057/9781137378477.0010

In general terms, pricing policies should be understood as the totality of decisions contributing to price setting of a product or service sold to the final consumer. These decisions depend on several determinants. It is not only the industrial cost of a given good or service to determine its final price. Modern pricing policies embrace, in addition to economic variables, a number of other factors, internal and external to the firm producing the good, and it often leads to setting a price that is dissociated from the production cost.

Pricing determinants may be divided in three major categories (Figure 5.2):

a) *economics* of a company – costs, risks and revenues;
b) *market demand* for that particular product;
c) *competition* – the number and behaviour of the competitors.

Narrowing pricing evaluation to the accounting items and the relationship between costs and revenues would simply confine the price analysis to a single dimension among the many adopted by modern pricing policies. In regards to modern enterprises, it is the combination of multiple factors that explains the pricing strategies and models, as well as the price level and structure, thus defining different typologies of price.

It is possible to affirm that, often, companies decide on prices which do not consider costs and potential revenues, even though the prices may still be consistent with the company's business strategies and

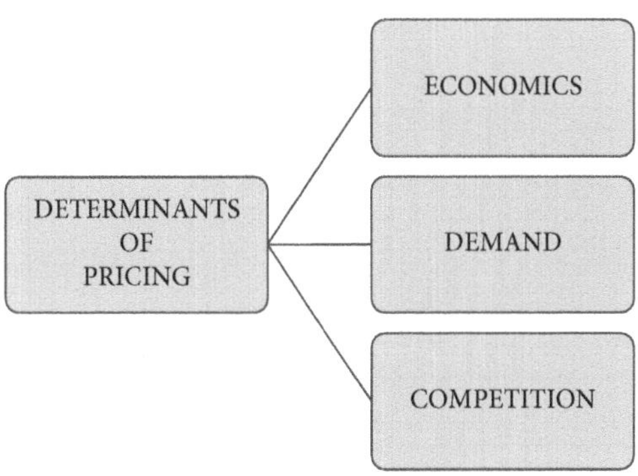

FIGURE 5.2 *Determinants of pricing*

DOI: 10.1057/9781137378477.0010

market dynamics. In brief, there are pricing policies dissociated from the economics of the product that:

a) determine profits, because they enable high sales volumes;
b) cause a negative balance between the product's costs and revenues, and still contribute to increasing the company's profits as they help to sell other products;
c) allow the achievement of strategic objectives, while causing a negative impact on balance sheet in the short term – as happens in the case of low price aimed at attacking a new market.

5.3 The economics of pricing

From purely economic and accounting point of view, the price of an audiovisual product should allow for the costs – both financial and operational – and the production risks, to be covered by the revenues deriving from selling a given quantity of the product and still generate a profit (Figure 5.3).
In analytical terms, it can be expressed as:

$$\text{price x quantity} = \text{costs} + \text{risks} + \text{mark-up} \qquad 5.1$$

and:

$$\text{price x quantity} = \text{revenue} \qquad 5.2$$

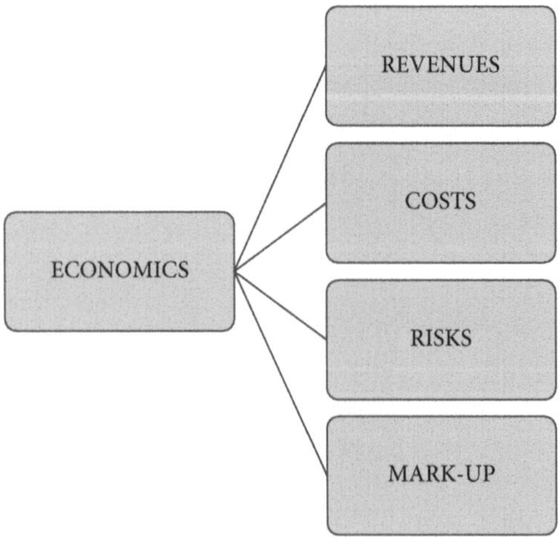

FIGURE 5.3 *The economics of pricing*

DOI: 10.1057/9781137378477.0010

the Formula 5.1 can also be expressed as:

$$revenues = costs + risks + mark\text{-}up \quad 5.3$$

or as:

$$sales\ revenues = operational\ costs + financial\ costs + risks\ costs + mark\text{-}up \quad 5.4$$

Price and costs

When defining a pricing policy it is important to take into consideration the cost of the product in the first place. Such an approach allows establishing what is called the "internal price" or the price calculated on the basis of the costs incurred by the producer without considering any market variable. According to this approach there are two types of internal prices:

- *floor price*:

  the *floor price* is the price that corresponds to the amount covering the direct costs;

- *break-even price*:

  the *break-even* price refers to the price that allows the company to recover total (direct and indirect) costs of a product. In this kind of estimation it is necessary to take into account the production volume in relation to what the overhead costs can be allocated. Since the *break-even* price depends on the product quantity, it is convenient for the producer to assume a range of values, from a *minimum* to a *maximum break-even price*, in relation to different estimated production volumes. In the case of audiovisual companies, the volume of production takes on a different connotation than that of other companies. Audiovisual companies produce *prototype goods*, one different from another, and therefore, the production volume coincides with the number of products, one different from another, realized in a year; moreover, instead of considering the number of units sold for each product, audiovisual firms take into account the number of right exploitations for any single product.

And therefore the major concern of an audiovisual company is to identify the price level that would cover both the direct costs and indirect costs attributable to that product. The greatest difficulty at this stage is that of an exact and precise estimation of costs.

DOI: 10.1057/9781137378477.0010

In this context, the production model chosen by a company and its size result in a different methodology and accuracy in estimating costs. In-house productions determine greater complexity of the allocation of indirect costs to a single product. The complexity increases proportionally to the complexity of the company itself. Most film production companies, for example, are small in size and often produce only one film a year. In such cases, the allocation of overhead costs does not pose particular problems. In the case of television companies, on the contrary, the structure's complexity and the large quantity of produced programmes make it more complex allocating overhead costs among different products. In the case of commissioned productions, a company delegates the production to a third party-producer. The direct costs agreed between the commissioning company and the executive producer are estimated accurately, item by item, while overhead costs faced by the executive producer are generally referred to as a lump sum.

Price and revenues

From an economic and accounting point of view, costs are offset by revenues. The difficulty of estimating the revenues from audiovisual products *ex ante* is caused by the unpredictability of the market response to the products and whether they will by appreciated by the audience. Therefore, it becomes complicated to estimate precisely the level of revenues and to foresee whether they will be sufficient at least to cover the costs. The economic literature defines the audiovisual product as an *experience good* – that is a good that finds its value/success in the experience of enjoyment of the consumer. This experience is unique and can be different also in respect to these products that have already been "tested" on the market – which is the case of remakes, sequels or of works inspired by previous productions that enjoyed a great success with the audience. Repeating a success can never be taken for granted.

There are examples in the American and Anglo-Saxon scientific literature of undertakings aimed at identifying quantitative methods useful to estimate the prospective revenues of a film. However, tests carried out on the proposed models did not lead to meaningful results, and the identification of a reliable model for forecasting film revenues to this day remains a challenge[1].

In order to manage the uncertainty of the revenue forecast, audiovisual companies fix a prudential revenue goal, that is, a rate of return large

DOI: 10.1057/9781137378477.0010

enough to compensate a possible negative variance between estimated and actual revenues. Economic determinants of pricing make audiovisual companies strongly profit-oriented; that leads to a tendency to add mark-up resulting in high final prices. High mark-up observed in the audiovisual industry is caused by the difficulty in estimating revenues.

Such an approach leads to defining a new category of internal price, the *target price*:

- *target price:*

  the target price corresponds to the price level which, in addition to covering direct and indirect costs, allows a company to achieve a desired profit. It is influenced by the assumed production volume. The profit margin can be expressed in relation to a particular return rate of the invested capital or, more simply, as a fixed margin to be added to the break-even price (mark-up).

Therefore, from an economic and accounting point of view, price can be expressed as (Formula 5.4 and Figure 5.4):

$$\textit{target price} = \textit{break-even price} + \textit{mark-up} \quad (5.4)$$

In the case of in-house productions, companies must estimate revenues and fix a profit rate. The market itself will then confirm or deny the accuracy of the forecast. If a company decides on commissioning a production, the costs will include the executive producer's fee. For the executive producer determining a price is less complicated. The costs will be agreed with the commissioning company, and revenues are

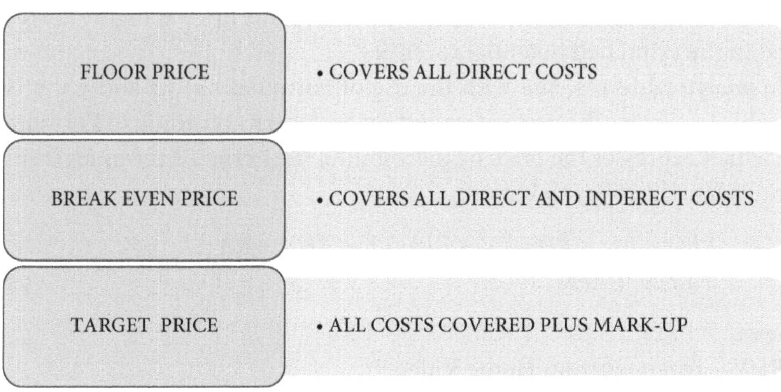

FIGURE 5.4 *Different dimensions of price*

DOI: 10.1057/9781137378477.0010

reflected by the fee, which is the mark-up. The fee depends, in large part, on the negotiating power of the counterparties. If the fee is too low, the commissioning company risks that the executive producer will be forced to reduce production costs, with potential harm to the quality of the final product. An excessively low fee, which is not consistent with the break-even price or the target price, puts the production at risk, creates a moral hazard on the part of the executive producer and may affect the quality of the product. In contrast, when the fee is too high, in addition to mark-up, it can also include a part of the overhead costs incurred by the executive producer, and the moral hazard of the executive producer occurs when the overhead costs include also those costs which are not directly attributable to the production.

Revenues, price and value of audiovisual products

The price of an audiovisual product can be considered an indicator of the value of the product itself. As the price incorporates the prospective revenue and desired profit, it is possible to say that the value of an audiovisual product is strongly dependent on revenue prospects on various exploitation markets.

As already explained, not all audiovisual products are able to access all national markets, and even fewer access foreign markets. Therefore, exploitation rights holders need to assess, on the basis of artistic and commercial features of the product, what are the potential revenues and which market to choose when orientating sales efforts. If it is true that the producer company will have to set a price which allows it to recover costs and make a profit, then it is also true that this price is highly correlated to the estimated potential revenues.

In analytical terms, and with the use of Formulas 5.1, 5.2 and 5.3, it is possible to express the price of an audiovisual work according to Formula 5.5, which expresses the price by discounting the expected revenues from various markets of exploitation:

$$P = Rbox\ office + RFreeTV + RPayTV + RHV + RA + RNM + RFM \qquad 5.5$$

where:

RHV = revenues from Home Video
RA = revenues from ancillary rights and derivatives
RNM = revenues from *New Media*
RFM = revenues from foreign markets.

DOI: 10.1057/9781137378477.0010

> The value of an audiovisual product is expressed by the discounted value of future revenues generated by the work on various markets of exploitation. This estimate is crucial to the fixing of the selling price of the product, as well as the price of the licensing of the exploitation rights.

As anticipated, the estimation of revenues of an audiovisual product contains some critical elements:

- it is subject to the audience approval of the product and therefore, attributable to an emotional experience that is difficult to assess *ex ante*;
- it refers to different channels of exploitation;
- it is differentiated for different territories, based on the forecasts of different responses from the audience;
- for each territory, the estimated revenue of the producer may differ with that of the local counterpart acquiring exploitation rights.

As the estimates of future revenues differ for different exploitation markets and territories, it can be stated that the same audiovisual work will have different prices on different exploitation markets and territories.

The difficulties arising from the forecast of revenues in different territories and in different markets of exploitation have forced professionals to look for empirical solutions inspired by their sense and experience, rather than from scientific models.

In order to deal with the forecasting difficulties, audiovisual companies use specific parameters to estimate the future *performance* of a product. For films primarily intended for cinema, it is common practice to consider such a parameter the revenues from ticket sales (*box office*). For television products, primarily or exclusively intended for television, the parameter is the *share*.

For films, the *box office* is the variable that mostly affects the sale price of all other rights of exploitation. When the sale is made before the film is released in the cinema, the price is set based on an estimate of the potential *box office*.

The *share* expresses the number of viewers counted while a television programme is being broadcasted. As it is calculated during the broadcast, for the purposes of presales, it is also necessary to estimate the *share ex ante*. The *share* of a feature film used for television exploitation, after being released in the cinema, is strongly influenced by the *box office*. There is a positive correlation between the *box office* and *share*. Most successful films (in terms of the *box office*) usually get high *share*.

DOI: 10.1057/9781137378477.0010

When the exploitation rights refer to foreign territories, estimating revenues is even more complicated, due to the fact that the *box office* and *share* recorded on the native market are less meaningful. Different tastes of audiences, from different territories, may contradict the success of a product in its country of origin. When it comes to the sale of rights for foreign territories for example, the established solution is to negotiate all possible exploitation rights; the negotiation of single rights occurs very rarely (i.e., television rights).

As the price is related to potential revenues, the buyer, rather than considering the value in use of the audiovisual work, considers the product as an investment. In this context, the valuation of price is influenced by three factors: (a) the present value of the future revenue at the time of negotiation; (b) the duration of the granted exploitation period; and (c) the frequency of use, referring to the number of opportunities for exploitation in the context of the negotiated period (Figure 5.5).

> The price of an audiovisual product depends on the estimated revenues, which are a function of the type of product, the exploitation period and frequency of use. Assuming other conditions being equal, the buyer is willing to pay a

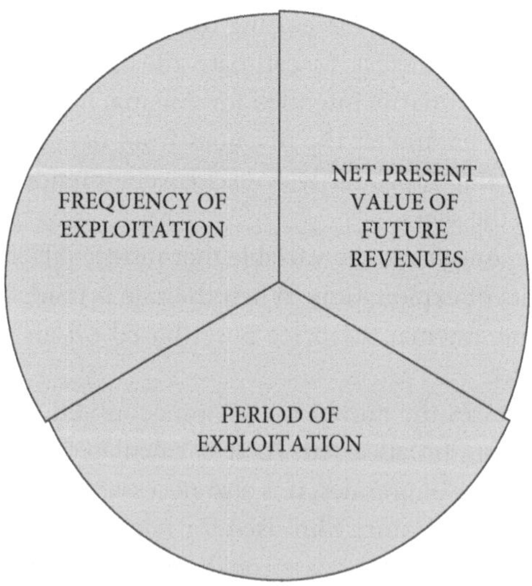

FIGURE 5.5 *Value, price and exploitation of audiovisual products*

DOI: 10.1057/9781137378477.0010

higher price for the same product if the period of exploitation is longer and the frequency of exploitation higher.

As an example, considering a film released in cinemas, the television rights for a period of five years will be worth less than those granted for 10 years, and the corresponding rights will have different prices. In this context, the maximum price coincides with the purchase of given rights in perpetuity. The extension of the exploitation period increases the volume of potential revenue. The number and opportunities of exploitation negotiated during the purchase of rights also affect the value of a product. This finding is particularly relevant for the television market where, in addition to the exploitation period, negotiations are also associated with the so-called "television runs", or the number of times that a film can be broadcasted. Finally, as the revenues are still only prospective; they must be discounted by a financial process that expresses the value of future revenues at the time of negotiation. Therefore, the choice of discount rate implies an additional choice that affects the price.

In conclusion, the price of an audiovisual product can be expressed as the present value of future revenues referred to individual markets of exploitation[2]. The value is a function of the period of assignment of rights (t) and negotiated television runs (p):

$$P(t, p) = Rbox\ office + RFreeTV + RPayTV + RHV + RA + RNM + RFM \qquad 5.6$$

Formula 5.6 is valid for all television programmes and films, but accessible exploitation markets and ways of exploitations should be evaluated for each product separately. Therefore, the Formula 5.6 will assume different configurations in relation to different products. For example, for products destined for the web, the expression of the price will be:

$$P\ web\ product\ (t, p) = RNM \qquad 5.6.1$$

More in general, the increasing co-existence of cross media products and linear and nonlinear media services will lead to a flexible conception of the Formula 5.6, which will be adapted to the specific feature of the product and its release.

As regards to the audiovisual market, the cost of production is scarcely indicative of the value of the products. The value is strongly dependent on potential revenues which, in turn, are a function of the

DOI: 10.1057/9781137378477.0010

distribution costs and, above all, of the response of the public. The positive correlation between production costs and revenue volume is not to be taken for granted and depends strongly on two specific elements, an economic one and a cultural one. In practice, it has been shown that it is not only the production budget that influences the success of a product, but also, and especially, the budget available for the promotion and launch of the product itself. American blockbusters, for example, have budgets to promote and launch almost equal to the cost of production. In Europe, on the contrary, the resources earmarked for the launch of a film are a small part of the industrial cost. In cultural perspective, it should be noted that, in the end, the success of the product is determined by the taste of the public, and the *audience* response is always uncertain and difficult to predict. It is often uncorrelated to the reputation of the actors and the director, and their previous successes. Several cases of high-budget films, with world-renowned casts, recording burning commercial disappointments, confirm what is stated above.

The fact that audiovisual products are "prototype" products, that their value depends mainly on the response of the audience, and that this is not predictable, results in the value estimation being a subjective judgment that cannot be verified, until after the airing of the product.

> To sum up, the price of an audiovisual product is poorly correlated to the production costs, and it is strongly correlated with the response of the public, the costs of promotion and launch and terms of use of the product itself. Being successful with the public is difficult to predict *ex ante*. The budget available for the promotion and the launch do not depend on the choices of production companies but are decided by the distribution companies. The ways of exploitation depend on the negotiation of the rights to the product. As a result, the price of audiovisual products: (a) cannot be related to objective parameters and (b) is a prototype price, or hardly comparable with the prices of other products, including those of similar technical and production features.

Not only economics

Pricing based on costs and revenues is only a starting point for determining the price of audiovisual products. Setting the price according solely to the economics may expose the production company to high risk of adopting inadequate *pricing* solutions.

DOI: 10.1057/9781137378477.0010

Since the *break-even price* and the *target price* are dependent on the number of products and on the markets of exploitation to which they have access, the lack of coincidence between what is assumed *ex ante* and the response of the market would lead to a methodology of "circular pricing" that is difficult to apply. Lower than expected audience response and number of exploitation markets would force the company to increase the price in order to maintain the same level of profit. Similarly, higher market response could result in price reduction. The difficulty of applying a "circular pricing" induces companies to incorporate in their pricing policies the variables referring to the market demand and the market's competitive structure.

5.4 Demand and pricing

Modern pricing policies are not oriented only to the internal dynamics of the firm – on the contrary, they take into account the needs of clients. In such perspective, it is relevant to analyse the demand from buyers before determining prices.

The company must identify its own target price that is compatible with the price accepted by the market. Prospective buyers of audiovisual products can be distinguished for product types. For television products, prospective buyers correspond to other broadcasters or distributors on other markets of exploitation, primarily Home Video and foreign markets. For films, the potential buyer is a film distribution company that will place the product on different markets of exploitation. Producers are rarely able to carry out sales on different markets themselves. For web products, placed freely on web platforms, there is no buyer of exploitation rights that remain with the filmmakers, or the sponsors in the case of branded products. And therefore there is no selling price. Platforms act as distributors without paying the purchase price, or acquiring ownership of the products. The following considerations will, therefore, be largely related to television products and films.

To consider the perspective of a potential buyer means to incorporate into the price three variables: *elasticity of demand*, *value and risk* perceived by the buyer, and the degree of *asymmetric information* between the production company and the buyer (Figure 5.6). Within the audiovisual market, these variables take on specific features that can strongly influence the price and the relative value of a product.

DOI: 10.1057/9781137378477.0010

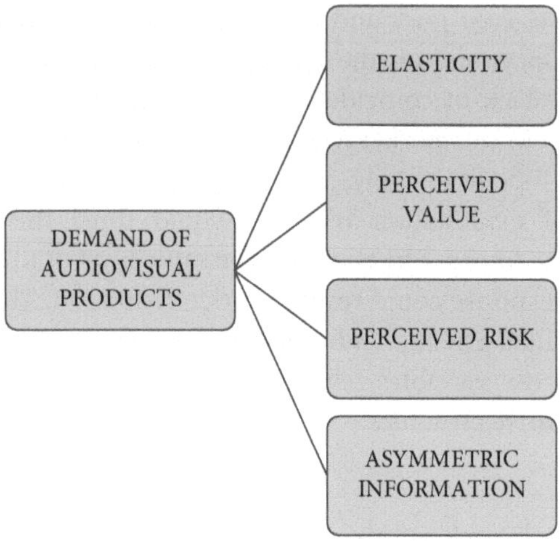

FIGURE 5.6 *Demand and pricing of audiovisual products*

The elasticity of demand

The sensitivity of the buyer in relation to the price is defined as "elasticity of demand". In economics, the elasticity is measured as a percentage change in the quantity of product purchased in relation to a percentage change in price of 1%. In conceptual terms, the buyer's reaction to the change in price shows how much the buyer is willing to pay in order to obtain a certain product. It can be affirmed that, the lower the price elasticity of the buyer, the less the buyer is willing to modify its purchase decision if the price increases.

Several econometric studies have highlighted the importance of the price elasticity and have detected the main factors affecting the behaviour of potential buyers of audiovisual products. Using the taxonomy proposed by Nagle and Holden (1994), it is possible to affirm that there are several variables that can explain the low elasticity of demand characterizing the market of audiovisual rights:

1 *Distinctive qualities of a product and the absence of substitute goods.* Audiovisual products are unique and not replicable. They are prototype goods and experience goods by nature, and therefore are not replaceable. For these reasons, the price sensitivity is generally low, especially among the broadcasters: once a particular product has been identified for a specific need of the programme schedule,

DOI: 10.1057/9781137378477.0010

it is complicated and expensive to find a suitable and comparable substitute.

2 *Advantages of a product.* The more a product is attractive and able to generate revenues, the lower is the sensitivity to its purchase price.
3 *Possibility of a combined investment.* This variable is of particular importance in the so-called "packaged sales", in other words, sales of a portfolio of rights relating to a given mix of titles. The basket of rights generally refers to titles of a different nature and appeal. The package includes both top quality titles and those of low appeal. However, the only way to purchase desired titles is to buy them together with those that are not "necessary". This negotiation practice results in a reduced price sensitivity of the buyer towards the less appealing titles.
4 *Stock-up effect.* The exploitation rights for audiovisual products are granted for a defined period of time, within which the buyer can use them to the extent agreed in the contract. The ability to dilute the exploitation of the purchased rights within the limits of time described in the contract results in a "stock-up effect" that lowers the price elasticity.

Therefore, the lower the demand elasticity in relation to the above-mentioned factors, the easier it will be for the selling company to manage the *technical price*. The company can more easily reconcile the *technical price* with profit goal, in the light of a lower sensitivity of the buyer towards the price, and set a higher *target price*.

> Low elasticity of demand helps to dissociate the price of an audiovisual product from economics. The lower it is, the higher is the applicable mark-up applied by the selling firm and, consequently, the greater the distance between target price and technical price.

Price and value perceived by the buyer

Variables that affect the demand elasticity lead to distinguishing a dimension of price referred to the buyer. More specifically, literature[3] distinguishes four price dimensions: "monetary price", "non-monetary price", "perceived price" and "perceived value" (Figure 5.7).

The *monetary price* expresses the financial costs incurred while purchasing the product. The *non-monetary* price includes also imputed costs of

DOI: 10.1057/9781137378477.0010

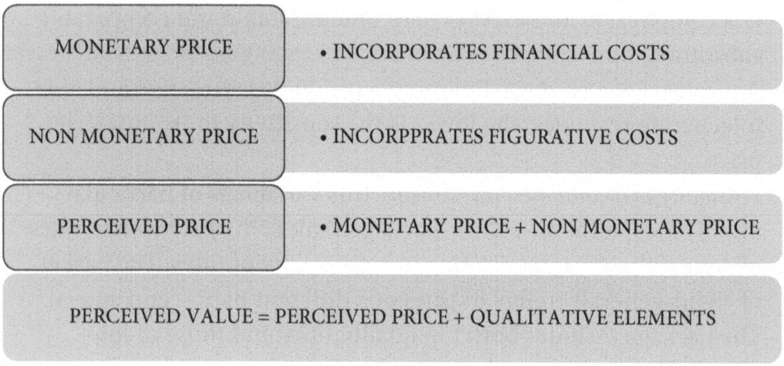

FIGURE 5.7 *Different dimensions of price for buyers*

time and energy, as well as the psychological costs associated with the purchase. Taken together, *monetary and non-monetary price* constitute the "perceived price" by the buyer. Therefore, the *perceived price* may be expressed as: *monetary price + non-monetary price*. The *perceived value* expresses the overall assessment that a consumer makes in relation to the usefulness of the product. The assessment considers not only the product – and its intrinsic and extrinsic features – but also different variables that determine its elasticity.

In their pricing policies, therefore, audiovisual companies should consider that, when deciding on a purchase, buyers not only take into account the *monetary price*, but also, and more likely, the *perceived value*. It is the perception of the overall value that makes buyers pay certain prices rather than others. If a broadcaster considers a programme crucial to its programme schedule, it will be willing to pay more due to a high *perceived value*. The concept of *perceived value* is definitely relevant for the audiovisual market because of the uniqueness of the product negotiated – rights of exploitation – and the nature of a prototype good of audiovisual products.

> The perceived value does not coincide with the monetary price and contributes to dissociate the price of a product from economic and accounting variables estimated by the selling company. The target price will deviate from the technical price also because of the value perceived by the customer. The higher the perceived value, the greater the applicable mark-up and, consequently, the distance between target price and technical price.

DOI: 10.1057/9781137378477.0010

Price and risk perceived by the buyer

The act of buying always involves taking risk by the buyer. In literature, the risk faced by the buyer has been divided into six categories: economic, psychological, performance, physical, social and global[4].

The economic risk refers to the risk of loss; the higher the purchase price, the higher the loss risk exposure. The psychological risk is due to emotional involvement and possible disillusionment that can come after the purchase. The risk of performance refers to the possibility of not achieving the expected result, considering the price paid for the product. The physical risk is linked to the deterioration of the purchased product. The social risk is due to the social value attributed to the possession of the purchased product. The global risk expresses the synthesis of different types of perceived risk.

Some research[5] identified the performance risk, the economic risk and the psychological risk as the top three among all the risks perceived by buyers.

As regards the audiovisual market, economic risk and performance risk have an impact on pricing because of the peculiarity of rights of exploitation and because audiovisual products are prototype goods of experiential nature. The performance risk, or the possibility of not getting the expected result from the product, is particularly highlighted.

> The lower the perceived risk, the greater the applicable mark-up and, consequently, the distance between target price and technical price.

Price and asymmetric information between buyer and seller

The difficulty in processing available information and what derives from the lack of information introduce a further influencing factor in pricing, namely the *asymmetric information* between the parties to the negotiations.

When the buyer is not in a position to evaluate, or obtain, the information necessary for purchase decisions, the price itself becomes an indicative value of quality.

Acquiring and processing available information requires from the buyer a specific *know-how* and time. Lack of time to acquire and process available information leads to a situation in which the consumer has difficulty in expressing the *perceived value* and, therefore, considers the price itself to be the indicator of the product value.

DOI: 10.1057/9781137378477.0010

> The lack of time and the unavailability of information lead to asymmetric information between buyer and seller. As a result, the price itself becomes an indicator of the product value and helps to distance the target price from the technical price (Wolinsky 1983). The less time available to the buyer, its know-how and available information, the greater the applicable mark-up and, consequently, the distance between target price and technical price.

On the market of television rights, asymmetric information works in more complex manner. It regards two aspects: the quality of the underlying product and the investment value of the product itself. The asymmetric information regarding the product quality is due to the fact that the purchase of rights regards products which have not yet been completed, or that have not been released to the public yet. This kind of asymmetry, for example, is typical of the *output contracts* and *volume deals* concluded by broadcasters directly with major film production companies[6]. It is common practice regarding these contracts that a broadcaster undertakes to purchase a package of products which include also the works that are not yet completed, and whose artistic value cannot be assessed yet.

The asymmetric information concerning the investment value refers to the knowledge gap between the parties regarding the revenues deriving from possible exploitations of rights by the buyer. A classic example is that of the purchase of foreign products. Hardly ever the rights owner can assess the potential revenue of the product on the buyer's market with the same accuracy as the buyer itself. In domestic trading, asymmetric information can be related to the existence of pre-agreement for future pre-sale contracts, but not known to the seller.

A multidimensional pricing model for buyers

The price-quality relationship, from the buyer point of view, leads to a multidimensional model of pricing taking into account different variables crucial to purchase choices. The elasticity of demand, the perceived value and risk, asymmetric information between sellers and buyers, are all elements that play a crucial role when making purchase decisions, and when deciding on the price one is willing to pay (Figure 5.8). Furthermore, the price itself often becomes, for the buyer, the most indicative quality indicator.

DOI: 10.1057/9781137378477.0010

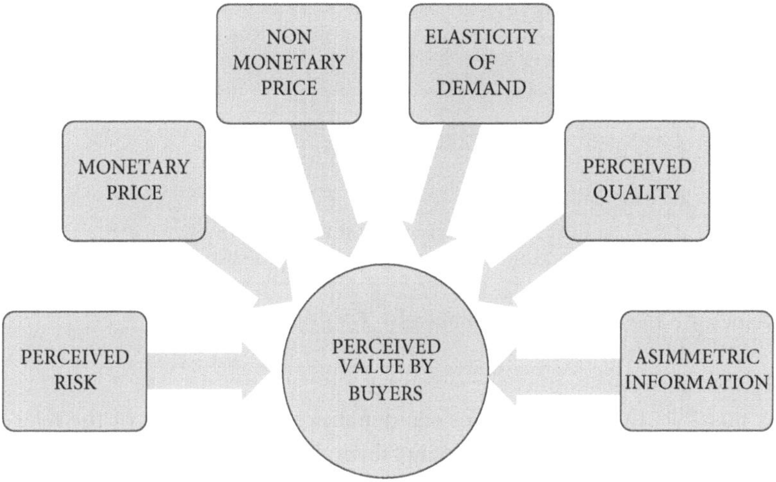

FIGURE 5.8 *The determinants of multidimensional price of buyers*

> The determinants of pricing, related to demand, can create economic space for the target price to distance itself from the technical price, allowing the selling companies to apply mark-up. As a result, the lower is the demand elasticity, the more significant are the perceived value, the asymmetric information and perceived risks the higher is the final price.

Similarly to what sellers do, buyers also set their own price range within which their purchasing decisions are made, narrowing the economic space for the pricing policies of the sellers. Several studies have shown that buyers are not willing to consider any purchase if the price exceeds the acceptable range. Such a price corridor, determined by the analysed variables, is marked by a minimum price ("buyer floor price") below which the quality perceived by the customer is too low, and by a maximum price ("buyer cap price") congruous with the revenue that can be allocated at the time of purchase. Within this range, it is possible to trace a "reference price" defined as the price on the basis of which the buyer evaluates all other prices (Figure 5.9).

> Economic space that the selling company can use for the purposes of setting the price, and its own mark-up, is limited by the price corridor with which the customer defines its reference price.

DOI: 10.1057/9781137378477.0010

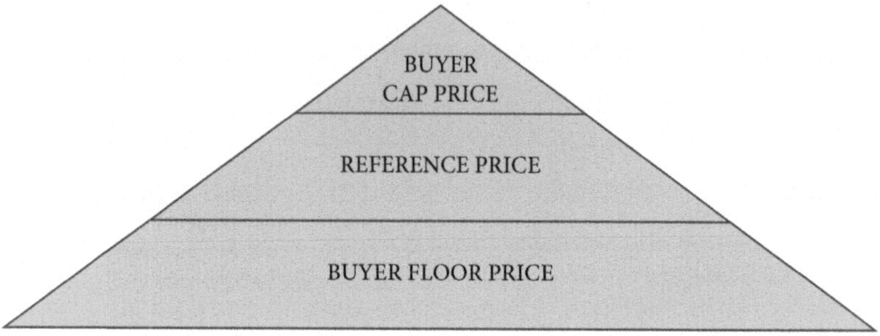

FIGURE 5.9 *The price corridor for buyers*

It is possible, therefore, to trace the dynamics of the setting of the *reference price* which develops following several steps: (a) determination of the *perceived value*, (b) determination of the *reference price*, (c) determination of the *acceptable price range* and (d) assessment of the price charged by the seller.

On the basis of the two major theories present in literature (*Adaptation Level Theory and Theory Assimilation-Contrast*) several studies were conducted[7] confirming that it is possible to construct the curves of the minimum and the maximum price and, therefore, the acceptable price corridor for a given product.

Therefore, when applying the mark-up and the final price, selling companies must adhere to the buyers' price corridor, if they want to avoid an increase in the price affecting the sale. The lower the price level, the lower the threshold of attention of the buyer; as a consequence the corridor of the buyer's price is less binding. In such conditions, the applicable mark-up, and the final price, can be higher and, consequently, the distance between the target price and the technical price will be larger.

When there is a well-established habit to buy certain goods, the valuation process is combined, and sometimes replaced, by the use of a "usual price"[8]. In essence, in such cases, the purchase decision is influenced more by a habit to pay a certain price, or at least a price fixed within a certain threshold: the *usual price* automatically becomes the *reference price*.

As regards the audiovisual market, the *reference price* and the *usual price* assume particular significance especially for the buying broadcasters.

> The frequency of purchase affects pricing. In conjunction with repeating purchases, the adoption of the usual price allows the selling companies, in

DOI: 10.1057/9781137378477.0010

the short- to medium-term, to maintain unchanged their mark-up margins and prices applied over time, regardless of the market performance.

5.5 Competition and pricing

Pricing policies find in the market structure an exogenous constraint that delimits the seller's pricing policy.

In particular, the intersection between two such variables, as perceived value and structural market conditions, determines four possible situations in which pricing assumes distinct features (Figure 5.10):

a) *high perceived value and small number of competitors* – this situation is similar to monopoly or differentiated oligopoly, in which the room for pricing policy is big: sellers can take advantage of the high value that the product has in the eyes of the customer, and at the same time do not have to worry about any other competitors.

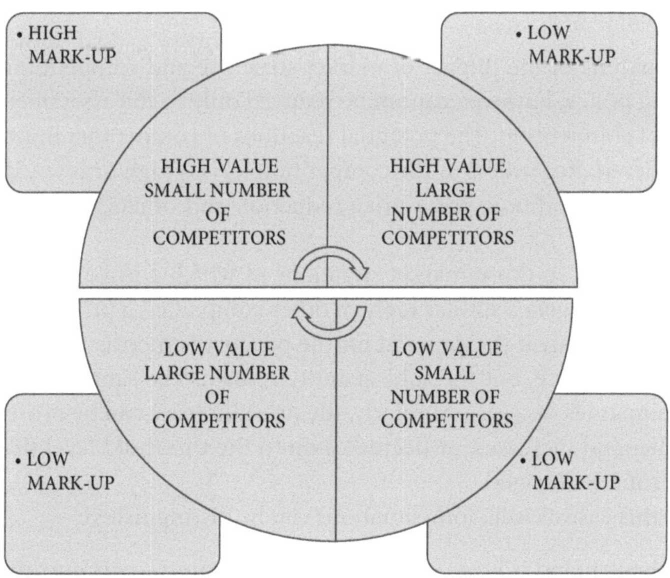

FIGURE 5.10 *Perceived value, competition and price*

Source: adapted from Lambin (2000).

DOI: 10.1057/9781137378477.0010

This situation can be associated with high mark-up and high final prices;

b) *low perceived value and large number of competitors* – this situation is opposite to the previous one and comparable to pure competition. In this case, the room for pricing policy is restricted, either because the customer does not perceive the product as highly differentiated and irreplaceable, or because of competitors' pricing policy. This situation can be associated with low mark-up and low final prices;
c) *low perceived value and small number of competitors* – this situation is similar to undifferentiated oligopoly. In this case, the degree of freedom in setting the pricing policy, which comes from a low level of competition, is limited by the low perceived value. This situation can be associated with low mark-up and low final prices;
d) *high perceived value and a large number of competitors* – this situation is similar to monopolistic competition. Also in this case, the autonomy of pricing exists because of strong product differentiation in the buyer's perception, but it is limited by the high competition. This situation can be associated with reduced mark-up and reduced final prices.

The analysis of the impact of market structure and competition on the pricing policy, however, cannot be reduced only to the assessment of the level of competition. The potential reactions of competitors must also be considered. Regardless of the competition level – high or low – there are favourable conditions for a price reduction and others favourable for a price increase[9].

For example, in those market situations in which a price change of one company triggers a similar reply of other companies, a price reduction is compatible only if the demand for the product is increasing. If all sellers reduce the price, but the sold quantity remains the same, the profits of all companies decrease. Similarly, the price increase can be prosecuted if the demand increases, or decreases up to the threshold level that leaves the profit unchanged.

In this case as well, four situations can be distinguished:

a) the demand is increasing and the competition reacts quickly;
b) the demand is increasing and the competition does not react;

DOI: 10.1057/9781137378477.0010

c) the demand is not increasing and the competition reacts;
d) the demand is not increasing and the competition does not react.

> Different market structures determine different degree of freedom for the company's pricing and have different impacts on the possibility to distance the target price from the technical price.

From an economic point of view, the situation (c) is favourable for neither a reduction nor an increase in price, since it will result in lower profits for the companies. In this case, a change in price could be justified only by other non-economic objectives.

> Different reactions of competitors, and different life cycles of the product, result in different degrees of freedom for a company's pricing policy and have different impacts on the possibility to distance the target price from the technical price.

A company which operates on different geographic markets finds itself to be operating within different market structures. And therefore it is possible that, for the same product, one company will have different margins in which to manoeuvre as regards to pricing. Such a condition allows applying different prices for the same product in different areas.

With reference to the European audiovisual industry, it is necessary to distinguish between the competitive structures of the TV market and that of the film market. The first one is generally comparable to a situation of oligopoly, with few large broadcasters that control the market; the latter to a model of pure competition, with many small-size producers. The value perceived by potential buyers changes in relation to the product, while the demand is generally not increasing and undergoes changes in relation to particular products, or in relation to short-term cycles. For this reason, it is not possible to place the audiovisual market in one of the quadrants of Figure 5.10. It is more a matter of situations that vary from sector to sector, and in relation to single products. However, there are some trends that can be identified as characteristic. For television products, a relatively low perceived value of a product on different exploitation markets – primarily Home Video and abroad – is associated to an oligopolistic supply structure. For film products, the supply structure is of competitive type and the perceived value is, on average, relatively low. As a result, with the exceptions of products of particular appeal, the competitive structure of the market contributes to a downward trend in the price.

DOI: 10.1057/9781137378477.0010

Naturally, different territories with different competitive structures, allow for different degrees of freedom for pricing policy and determine different gaps between the target price and the technical price, depending on the geographic market.

Price increases may be motivated by contingent competitive dynamics, as referred to particular markets and particular historical contexts. The development of private national and local broadcasters recorded in Europe since the 1980s has generated an increased demand on television products and films. Broadcasters not only had to cover the urgent needs of programming, but also chased successful products in order to take market share from their competitors and to consolidate their own position on the market. In those years, therefore, there was a substantial increase in the prices of audiovisual products, both domestic and international – mainly American. This increase was generalized and transferred also on products with relatively low perceived value that could enjoy the "pulling effect" independent of their own characteristics.

5.6 Structure and level of price

Structure and level of price are strongly correlated elements. The structure is defined by the quantity and quality elements that make up the price: they define the price level. The price level has different meanings: an internal one, referring to the selling company, and two external ones, referring respectively to demand and competition.

The price structure is defined by the sum of the explicit and implicit components that are incorporated into the final price applied to consumers.

Explicit components are represented by quantitative elements expressed by direct and indirect costs; they determine, namely, the *threshold price* and the *break-even price*. Implicit components are due to all those variables that contribute to distance the final price from the *break-even price* and to set the *target price* – including not only the desired profit rate, but also the qualitative components related to demand and competition.

Two algebraic dimensions of price can be distinguished, corresponding to two meanings: the quantitative one and the qualitative one:

DOI: 10.1057/9781137378477.0010

price = amount of money transferred by the purchaser / quantity of goods sold by the seller 5.7

price = monetary and non-monetary sacrifices of the buyer / customer's satisfactions 5.8

The net effect of the profit rate and quality components lead to a new definition of an "*applied target price*":

applied target price = break-even price + mark-up + qualitative variables 5.9

In this perspective, the selling company can charge a price – the *applied target price* (or the *final price*) that can be higher or lower than the *target price.*

The applied target price may deviate from the target price on the ground that the mark-up not only incorporates the technical profit rate, but also the qualitative elements that can be algebraically added to it to determine positive and negative differences.

Finally, the *final price* is influenced by the "trigger prices" that configure specific manoeuvre corridors for pricing. These *trigger prices* relate to the direct cost of the production, the *reference price* of the buyer and the prices charged by competitors (Figure 5.11).

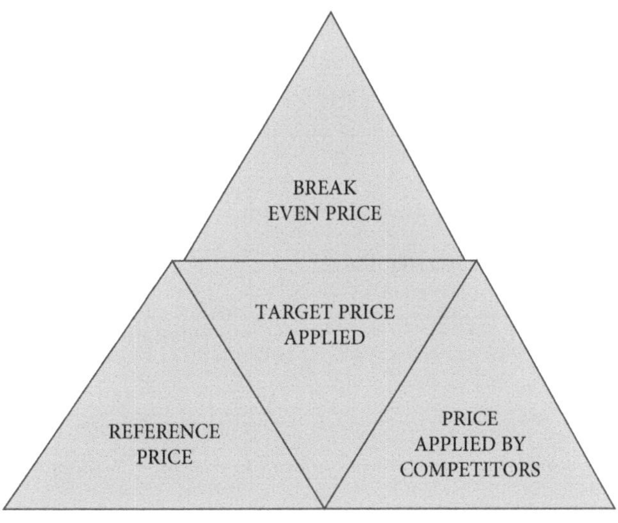

FIGURE 5.11 *The corridor of applied target price*

DOI: 10.1057/9781137378477.0010

The level of price, therefore, is different for the different dimensions of the price and, with reference to the *final price* (*applied target price*), is affected by the complexity of the price structure defined by a variety of quantitative and qualitative components considered by the selling company in accordance with the pricing policy adopted.
On the audiovisual rights market, given the nature of right of exploitation, it is common that the *target price* is far from the *applied target price.*

5.7 Pricing models

In relation to the above mentioned, it is possible to identify four main pricing models for audiovisual products. Companies may adopt as a reference the individual price of a single product, or the price of a basket of products – these two pricing models are called "product pricing" and "package-based pricing". In this way the pricing model, chosen by the company according to its strategy, defines the priority variable that inspires the price: a single product or a package (Figure 5.12).

On the audiovisual market, usually a combination of product-based models and packaged-based models can be observed. The former are found chiefly on the film market, characterized by small size production

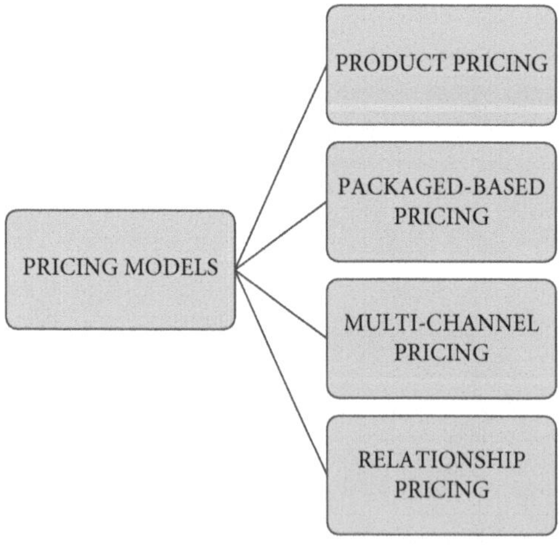

FIGURE 5.12 *Pricing models*

DOI: 10.1057/9781137378477.0010

companies able to place on the market one product at a time; on the television market, on the contrary, it is common to track prices referred to a portfolio of titles.

In addition, the pricing models can be affected by the market of rights exploitation (*multi-channel pricing*) and inspired by customer relationship (*relationship pricing*).

Notes

1 Eliashberg & Shugan 1997; Basuroy, Chatterjee & Ravid 2003; Doshi & Krauss 2010; Foutz & Jank 2010.
2 The theoretical framework does not take into account the phenomenon of piracy, which impacts negatively on net revenues potentially arising from the success of the product.
3 Costabile, 1992; Zeithaml, 1988.
4 Jacoby & Kaplan (1972).
5 Kaplan, Zybillo & Jacoby (1974).
6 For more details on output and volume deals, see chapter 7.
7 Stoetzel 1954; Adam 1958; Gabor & Granger 1961, 1965; Monroe 1971.
8 Valdani (1986).
9 Porter (1983).

DOI: 10.1057/9781137378477.0010

OPEN

6
The Value of Audiovisual Firms

Abstract: *Assessments of audiovisual firms are complicated by the specificity of the industry; the value of an audiovisual firm is related to the commercial exploitation of the audiovisual products for which the company holds the relevant rights. Traditional assessment methods, therefore, should be properly adapted to the specific nature of the business. The methodologies for evaluating audiovisual firms focus on the assessment of their exploitation rights, and their estimated values coincide with the value of their libraries of exploitation rights. This chapter proposes an evaluation model specifically dedicated to audiovisual firms, based on "cash flow method". The chapter highlights also some criticalities of the flow-based method and suggests some corrections to be applied to the standard methodology.*

La Torre, Mario. *The Economics of the Audiovisual Industry: Financing TV, Film and Web.* Basingstoke: Palgrave Macmillan, 2014. DOI: 10.1057/9781137378477.0011.

 DOI: 10.1057/9781137378477.0011

6.1 Introduction

The need to estimate the value of a firm is generally related to major financial transactions. In regard to the ordinary activities of firms, their estimated value can be requested for financing purposes by lenders who need to carry out creditworthiness analysis, determine the sustainability of the credit or demand specific guarantees. Firm evaluation is instead mandatory when dealing with extraordinary business operations – such as sales, mergers, transfer of share packages and extraordinary procedures such as bankruptcy.

Their theoretical value, determined through the use of specific methods, is generally adjusted through a number of subjective evaluations related to specific operational needs; in case of major transactions such as mergers and acquisitions, the estimated value constitutes the basis for negotiating the final price.

Assessments of audiovisual firms are complicated by the specificity of this sector; traditional assessment methods, therefore, should be properly adapted to the specific nature of the business. Evaluations of audiovisual firms are not common – given their reduced access to credit and rare use of structured finance – and, generally, are performed with methods based on financial flows.

With a view of encouraging a greater interaction between the financial system and the audiovisual industry, assessment of such firms represents an essential element, especially to facilitate their access to credit. For such purpose, this chapter intends to propose an evaluation model specifically dedicated to audiovisual firms, based on what the literature defines as "cash flow method". The analysis of the methodology is accompanied by the description of the evaluation process. Finally, the chapter highlights also some criticalities of the flow-based method, in light of the current and future market dynamics, and suggests some corrections to be applied to the standard methodology.

6.2 Evaluating a firm: which methodology for the audiovisual industry?

Literature and business practice have explored several business evaluation methods, with the aim of using the ones that best fit the single operations at issue.

DOI: 10.1057/9781137378477.0011

Regardless of the methodology for such evaluation, the value of an audiovisual firm is related to the commercial exploitation of the audiovisual products for which the company holds the relevant rights. Audiovisual firms, in fact, with a few exceptions, generally do not diversify their activities through investments in real or financial assets, nor are they characterized by high levels of traditional assets.

> The methodologies for evaluating audiovisual firms, therefore, focus on the assessment of their exploitation rights. Hence, their estimated economic value must coincide with the value of their libraries of commercial exploitation rights.

Exploitation rights of audiovisual products are neither real nor financial assets, instead they fall under the category of the so-called "intangible assets". Here we distinguish between detectable and non-detectable assets; following a traditional definition, the former are related to specific financial assets (e.g., credits or deposits), while the latter relate to different factors, such as human capital, management quality, image or reputation of firms in their reference markets, and constitute what is commonly defined as "goodwill". Audiovisual exploitation rights fall under the category of the detectable intangible assets and are related to the exploitation of assets represented by the audiovisual products (Figure 6.1).

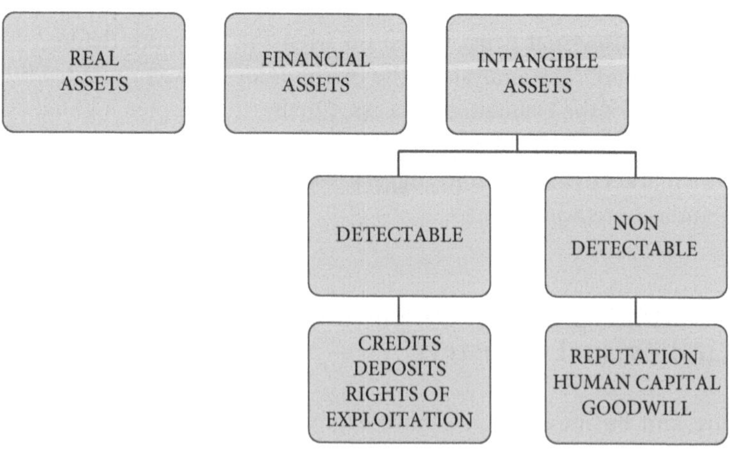

FIGURE 6.1 *The nature of exploitation rights*

DOI: 10.1057/9781137378477.0011

The estimate of the value of audiovisual firms, therefore, must follow methodologies used to assess intangible assets. Here, the literature identifies three options that are widely used in the common business practice: cash flow-based method, cost-based method and market-based method.

Cash flow-based models regard assets as investments and determine their value by discounting the cash flows generated. Generally speaking, therefore, according to these models, the formula indicating the value of the assets is expressed by the sum of the discounted cash flows (FL) and final asset values (Wn)

$$FL = (FLn1) / (1+i) + (FLn2) / (1+i)^{\circ} .... + (FLn\ n) / (1+i)^{\circ} + Wn / (1+i)^{\circ} \quad 6.1$$

Cash flow-based models, therefore, equal the asset value to the present cash flow value; cash flows are represented by the difference between revenues and costs (earnings method) or income and expenditures (financial method). In the case of libraries of exploitation rights related to audiovisual products, the inflows generated by the rights originate from the different forms of exploitation of such products on the market, while the outflows are given by various costs related to distribution or overhead *pro rata* costs of the single products.

However, within these models, we can further distinguish between different methods according to the nature of the flows and the capitalization regime. Specifically, we distinguish methods that take into account specific cash flows within a given period or, in case it is impossible to estimate the exact amount, methods based on normalized expected cash flows. As for the capitalization regime, we can differentiate between methods considering an unlimited number of flows and applying a perpetual capitalization regime, and methods that adopt a limited capitalized regime.

For libraries of audiovisual products, the preferred method of choice is the limited capitalized regime, generally to ten years, while to determine cash flows, the professionals in the sector adopt mostly a mixed method based on both specific estimates and standard values following specific parameters.

The methodology at issue, however, imposes two additional choices: one is related to the expected cash flow growth rate; the other concerns the discount rate.

In both cases, the market practice adopts a highly conservative approach that tends not to incorporate any cash flow growth rate and

DOI: 10.1057/9781137378477.0011

considers a specific risk premium for this sector when determining the discount rate.

Cost-based methods match the value of the assets with the cost attributable to them; besides real asset activities, they include also intangible assets, such as, for instance, trademarks, patents, rights, human capital and know-how. Here, we can distinguish three criteria: adjusted historical cost, replacement or reproduction cost and loss cost.

The historical cost method determines the value of the assets according to their production cost, aptly adjusted in order to incorporate a possible depreciation of the assets. The replacement or reproduction cost method calculates the value of an asset according to the cost needed to acquire a similar one; *de facto*, this method consists of discounting the investment necessary to produce an equivalent asset capitalized for a period of time needed to produce the asset itself.

The *loss cost method* determines the value of an asset by discounting the difference between the cash flows that the firm would receive if it had the asset and those resulting from the loss of the same. It is based on specific balance sheet values.

Finally, the *market or empirical methods* determine the value of the asset through a number of market indicators. Such methods revolve around some specific ratios related to firms operating in the same industry and of similar size (*Price/Cash Flow*, *Price/Sales*, *Enterprise Value/Earnings Before Interest, Taxes or Enterprise Value/Earnings Before Interest*, *Taxes*, *Depreciation/Amortization*) with the extrapolation of an average value, which, compared with the company's balance sheet, will show the estimated value of the economic capital of the firm.

The choice of the most suitable methodology to represent the value of the assets examined must be carried out with the intent of maximizing the rationality, objectivity and neutrality of the evaluation. In other words, the value assigned to the assets must originate from a logical and consequential process (rationality), based on reliable and, if possible, verifiable data (provability) and without being affected by the distorting effects related to specific market dynamics or commercial relationships characterized by bargaining power circumscribed in space and time (neutrality).

The *cash flow-based method* appears to be the most suitable to determine the value of audiovisual libraries, as it is consistent with the above-mentioned criteria; it is also the most used by business practice. Cost-based methods do not suit audiovisual products, which, as prototypes, do not

DOI: 10.1057/9781137378477.0011

allow for a direct correlation between value and cost. Following market-based methods, the assessment outcomes are obviously influenced by the choices made on the type of assets examined and the price selected. Moreover, the audiovisual industry has a very few benchmarks, mostly referred to the American market and, therefore, hardly compatible with national European and extra-EU markets.

On the other hand, cash flow-based methods allow taking into account the specific nature of audiovisual products as well as their libraries; they also facilitate compliance with the afore-mentioned criteria of rationality, objectivity and neutrality. The flexibility of this method allows combining specific estimates, where necessary and possible, with standardized values; the business practice has consolidated approaches that tend to limit the capitalization period, ignore any flows growth rate under the period examined and incorporate a specific risk premium for the sector. These factors ensure a prudential estimate and a customization of the evaluation.

6.3 Evaluating a library of audiovisual products

Defining the potential markets for future inflows

To determine the value of audiovisual libraries, the second step in the process involves the choice of the exploitation markets to consider (Figure 6.2).

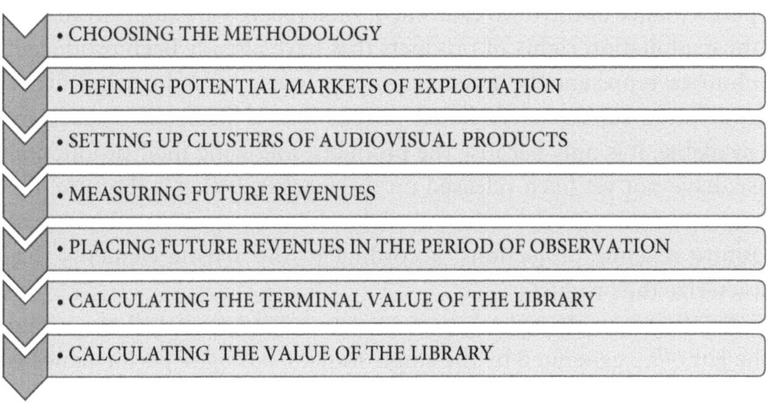

FIGURE 6.2 *The steps to evaluate a library*

DOI: 10.1057/9781137378477.0011

Given the specific nature of audiovisual products, the evaluation should take into account multiple markets; regarding cinematographic work, for instance, the most logical choice is to include all exploitation markets; television products instead should be assessed by selecting specific markets according to historical exploitation data, as per normal practice. In other cases, libraries may include exploitation rights related to a variety of different products; in such cases, the evaluation shall necessarily cover all exploitation markets, even if some of them will only involve some specific products.

A non-restrictive approach, therefore, should generally consider the following exploitation markets: Theatrical, Home Video (HV), Pay TV (Pay), Pay Per View (PPV), Video on Demand (VOD), Free TV (Free), New Media (NM), Accessories (Remake-Prequel-Sequel and Spin-off), Ancillary markets, foreign markets.

Setting up clusters of audiovisual products

Once the reference markets have been established, we need to decide which parameters to use to measure the future cash flows related to the single library products.

The next step consists of setting up clusters of audiovisual products within the libraries. The latter are divided into different categories, where audiovisual products are classified. The categories identify different kinds of potential to generate revenues; top categories are assigned higher revenue projections. Classes and the classification of audiovisual products are determined according to the historical records related to the performance of the titles examined; such records are surely available, for the exploitation rights of products that have already been produced. As libraries represent the most important assets of audiovisual firms, the evaluation cannot cover future production. If historical records are not available, it is only because the products, following their production phase, have not yet been released on the market. If this is the case, the placement of such products in one of the above categories will be based on future revenue projections, according to the artistic elements that characterize the products.

As for cinema works, title clusters are determined, first of all, according to the *box office* generated by the single movies: *box office* performance is considered a significant benchmark to calculate the commercial potential of a given product also in other exploitation markets. Alternatively,

DOI: 10.1057/9781137378477.0011

in order to avoid distortions related to different tickets prices over time, also in light of inflation rate, another option is to consider the number of viewers (tickets sold).

As for TV products, as well as all other products not expected to be released on the big screen, the reference economic parameter is given by the advertising revenues that can be associated to the products; alternatively, if the above data is absent, we can consider the *share*, as an audience measurement technique.

Products characterized by highly cultural content, whose performance obviously cannot be measured only according to strictly economic parameters, are generally included in a category of their own. This is the case of documentaries, for instance.

The clusters' thresholds are determined following data related to the single titles examined and, therefore, may vary according to the libraries. In general, it is necessary to identify clusters ensuring a limited dispersion of the revenue values observed. The number of quality grids may vary depending on the evaluations; in case of composite and comprehensive libraries, at least four clusters should be distinguished:

- *Top class A*, representing the firms' cutting-edge products, those with high commercial potential, in any case higher than the market average;
- *Class A*, including all titles that obtained revenues lower than Top Class A products, but still relevant; this class represents high-profile products with good commercial potential, in any case higher than the market average;
- *Class B*, representing titles that generated lower revenues than Class A products; this class includes the so-called "support" titles, those with discrete commercial potential, in line with the market average.
- *Bottom class C* includes titles that generated minimal revenues and characterized by limited commercial potential; this class represents the lowest value in terms of expected revenue streams from marketing.

It must be pointed out that the placement of the titles in grids according to the parameters chosen may be subject to some corrections. For some titles, it might be necessary to carry out specific analysis in order to obtain a more accurate classification; sometimes, in fact, values in terms of exploitation rights may not be related to the *box office* figures or TV *share*. Such corrections may be due to artistic and commercial

DOI: 10.1057/9781137378477.0011

reasons related to different factors, such as the participation in festivals and awards received, the reputation of the directors or the cast – or their unexpected artistic and commercial success – the international success of the titles or the rediscovery of some genres that determines a sudden increase of their value.

The methodology to estimate future revenues

Once the clusters for the single library products have been identified, the next step is to choose the methods to determine estimated revenues related to the different forms of future commercial exploitation.

First of all, cash flows must be considered according to the percentages of exploitation rights held by the firms; some titles, in fact, may be co-produced or purchased only after production; in such cases, a firm can only hold a percentage of their exploitation rights or rights only for some specific markets and only for a limited period. Assessors, therefore, should carefully verify the ownership of the exploitation rights for each single product, their percentages, the holding period and exploitation markets.

Cash flow assessment must highlight a picture of the flow of funds actually available. Generally, cash flow projections are considered gross of production and acquisition costs, as well as overhead costs – for the latter have already occurred at the assessment date – and net of distribution costs and commissions – if not incurred. Regarding cinema works, we therefore need to subtract the revenues due to distributors and exhibitors from the expected cash flows generated by their theatrical release.

In each exploitation market, then, we should divide between first sales and subsequent sales (mainly second and third sales) of the exploitation rights. To determine the value of the former, the benchmark could be represented by the amounts indicated in the contracts entered by the firms, or by market data, if available. Any time firms have in place contracts on the titles examined, the reference revenues are those expressed in the contracts: of course, here we should only consider revenue flows not yet collected at the time of the evaluation.

In some markets, such as Pay TV, there are official parameters to determine the value of the rights: it is not uncommon that Pay TV broadcasters adopt "escalators" to calculate the standardized purchase price of audiovisual rights; for films released at cinemas, the escalators' benchmark is represented by the *box office* results. Be advised that the prices indicated in the escalators, though constituting a significant

DOI: 10.1057/9781137378477.0011

reference basis, may significantly differ from the actual negotiation prices, due both to the number of runs planned and the exploitation period planned, and also to package sales, where the single titles are usually sold at flat rates, often a much more convenient system than selling them separately. It is up to the discretion of the assessors to evaluate the capacity of the single titles to access the exploitation markets considered; especially for the lower library clusters, it may be savvy to adopt a prudential approach and rule out some exploitation forms. When titles express no significant independent potential, but could be included in package sales, it is possible to indicate a standardized value for the whole category for some markets. Here too the assessors' discretion plays a relevant role.

As for second sales on different exploitation channels, in general, the most widespread methodology determines the revenues by reducing first sale revenues by a given percentage. Usually, low percentage reductions are applied to top categories, then they gradually increase for the bottom quality grids. These percentages of reduction will be even higher in case of further sales following the second. In this case too, it may be appropriate to rule out revenues for some specific titles or categories; again, it is in the assessors' discretion to establish the commercial potential of the products over time.

The distribution of future revenues

Expected future revenues must be considered over a period of time; it is, therefore, necessary to establish the evaluation reference period. As anticipated, generally, the audiovisual industry relies on a ten-year period; according to standard contracts, we can assume that titles can be exploited up to the third sale. It goes without saying that each title has a different commercial potential in different markets and, therefore, not all titles and categories can be evaluated throughout a complete sales cycle.

The estimated cash flows have to be distributed over the evaluation reference period following a prudential approach. In particular:

- for the temporal placement of the first sales, we need to consider a physiological time frame for relatively new titles, while it is appropriate not to include in the evaluation future revenues related to the oldest library titles that, at the time of assessment, have not yet accessed some exploitation markets;

DOI: 10.1057/9781137378477.0011

- for the temporal placement of the second sales, it is appropriate to consider a break following the first sale, assuming that firms are not able to immediately renegotiate their rights; and
- as for the third sales, a prudential approach would suggest to place them at the end of the period, regarding them as residual opportunities to generate less significant revenues for evaluation purposes.

The terminal value of the library

In addition to the expected revenues, the assessment considers also a "terminal value" of the whole library at the end of the exploitation period. Such expectation is justified by the firms' going-concern, which is taken as a fundamental assumption in the methodology of choice. This value is included on the assumption that firms will continue to operate also following the period considered by the evaluation.

Of course, the terminal value can only be referred to products for which the firms hold perpetual ownership/co-ownership rights. Following a prudential approach, this method does not consider the exploitation of temporary license rights over periods following the evaluation reference period.

The terminal value of libraries at the end of the evaluation reference period is generally calculated by applying a percentage reduction only to the value of the titles owned; the terminal value will be much lower as far away as is the last year of assessment in question, and the more intense and repeated the cycle of exploitation adopted for the estimate.

The value of the library

Once we have identified the future cash flows originating from the libraries, we must proceed to discounting according to the observation period chosen. The discount rate is established by considering, first of all, a benchmark rate for the risk-free rate; generally, the most popular benchmarks are the interest rates paid by government bonds with duration equal to, or close to, that of the evaluation period. A premium for general enterprise risk is added to the risk-free rate. Following a prudential approach, given the intangible nature of the assets at issue and the volatility expressed by the audiovisual market – a further specific risk premium can be added.

DOI: 10.1057/9781137378477.0011

The risk-free rate and the risk premiums are determined by the assessors on an individual basis and vary according to the economic cycle, as well as the specific economic cycle of the industry.

The sum of future revenue flows and the library terminal value, discounted at the rate established, shall determine the library value. For economic and strategic evaluation purposes, this value can be broken down in relation to both the clusters and the exploitation markets considered (Tables 6.1 and 6.2). In the first case, the assessment allows identifying the quality composition of the portfolio of rights held by

TABLE 6.1 *Value of the library by class of products*

CLUSTERS	NET PRESENT VALUE
TOP CLASS A	
TOTAL TOP CLASS A	
CLASS A	
CLASS B	
CLASS C	
DOCUMENTARY	
TOTAL VALUE FUTURE REVENUES	
TERMINAL LIBRARY VALUE	
TOTAL LIBRARY VALUE	

TABLE 6.2 *Value of the library by exploitation markets*

MARKETS OF EXPLOITATION	NET PRESENT VALUE
THEATRICAL	
PAY	
PPV	
VOD	
HV	
FREE	
NEW MEDIA	
ANCILLARY	
FOREIGN MARKETS	
REMAKE, PRE-SEQUEL E SPIN-OFF	
DOCUMENTARY	
TOTAL VALUE REVENUES PER MARKETS	
TERMINAL LIBRARY VALUE	
TOTAL LIBRARY VALUE	

DOI: 10.1057/9781137378477.0011

firms; further examinations may help determine the technical, artistic and economic characteristics of the titles included in the different classes.

The classification based on exploitation markets offers indications on the business capabilities of the firms, as well as the commercial potential of the products in their portfolios.

In general, besides the quantitative data summarized by the library value, the evaluation can provide useful qualitative indications for the strategic repositioning of products and firms alike.

Some critical issues

The evaluation methodology described aims to determine the library value of firms; as a portfolio of exploitation rights often represent the main asset – if not the sole asset – of a given audiovisual firm, library evaluation can be considered a proxy of the audiovisual firm assessment as a whole.

However, the recent market dynamics impose a critical rethinking of the methodologies currently used to estimate the value of audiovisual libraries in the business. These methods, in fact, have been used too mechanically. The division of the titles in clusters inevitably results in a standardized evaluation of titles belonging to the same cluster. This solution, which is useful in case of libraries composed of a variety of titles, clashes with the very "nature" of the "exploitation rights" as intangible assets. The assets underlying exploitation rights are audiovisual products, which are prototypes by definition; in light of this, it is reasonable to assume that each title may have its own commercial history that cannot be assessed through standardized parameters.

The choice of the evaluation period itself, which tends to consider medium- and long-term opportunities for exploitation, while being consistent with the exploitation cycle of audiovisual products, clashes with market volatility. The economic crisis has clearly showed that the value of assets – whether real, financial or intangible assets – is subject to economic cycles and characterized by significant degrees of volatility. Although audiovisual is one of the most uncorrelated businesses from the traditional sectors, some of its internal financial dynamics make it vulnerable to economic cycles. In particular, all those products for which the biggest source of revenues is constituted by their exploitation on the TV market are heavily exposed to the performance

DOI: 10.1057/9781137378477.0011

of advertising, and through this, to the economic cycles of the single countries. Consequently, any time future revenues are estimated on overly extended periods of time, the risk is to lose the significance of the estimate and obtain misleading indications.

In this perspective, the very same definition of discount rate might be denied in the short term. The interest rate trends recorded in different countries and main economic areas in recent years call for increasingly prudential choices.

Audiovisual libraries' and firms' evaluations are needed to facilitate a convergence process between the financial markets and the audiovisual industry. It is, therefore, necessary to push for a library-oriented culture and proper evaluation methods. Markets, though, should promote tailor-made evaluation methods to a greater degree; audiovisual products must be treated as prototype assets indeed, whose commercial potential is related to the efficiency of the distribution chain and the emotional response from the public. A greater attention on the single titles, precise reconstruction of historical data and a more flexible articulation of the clusters may all help achieve tangible benefits for evaluation purposes.

On the other hand, it must be pointed out that medium- and long-term evaluation perspectives do not fit the nature of the industry and its interactions with the economic system. It is, therefore, necessary to adjust the evaluation to the individual cases and adopt an increasingly prudential approach as much as the observation period is extended, along with more frequent updates of the estimate.

DOI: 10.1057/9781137378477.0011

OPEN

7
The Financial Model of the Audiovisual Industry

Abstract: *All audiovisual sectors are characterized by financial models which only in rare circumstances refer to intermediaries and to financial markets. Financial sources come from, primarily, public funds and from the pre-sales of copyrights to other businesses of the industry.*

This chapter describes the most adopted models of negotiation of copyrights exploitation in the audiovisual industry, differentiating the television, film and web sectors. Being the financial sources correlated to pre-sales of future profits, the chapter analyses the different sales agreements between majors and broadcasters, and the distribution deals between distributors and independent producers.

La Torre, Mario. *The Economics of the Audiovisual Industry: Financing TV, Film and Web*. Basingstoke: Palgrave Macmillan, 2014. DOI: 10.1057/9781137378477.0012.

 DOI: 10.1057/9781137378477.0012

7.1 Introduction

The financial model of the audiovisual industry changes in relation to the sector and to the type of product. Financial sources come from, primarily, other businesses of the sector or from public funds. And only in rare circumstances does the term refer to intermediaries and to financial markets. Nevertheless, television, cinema and web sectors have developed financial models which mark themselves in relation to the nature of the market players and to the features of the products. Broadcasters find their primary source of financing in selling advertising time, even if public broadcasters can also count on state financing and, with pay TV, on subscription fees. Movie producers avail themselves of public funds and pre-sales of copyrights exploitation managed by distribution companies that, often, anticipate a quota of the sales to the producers. Filmmakers active on the web do not adopt a structured financing model; considering that the greatest section of the native web audiovisual products are self-financed, financial dynamics related to the web are conditioned by the nature of the product. OTT services active in the web market are adopting the same dynamic of broadcasters, catalysing resources through advertising and subscription fees.

The assumption behind the different financial models is that audiovisual products can generate revenues in relation to copyright exploitation. In the light of the above, this chapter focusses on the most adopted models of negotiation of copyrights in the audiovisual industry, differentiating the television, movie and web sectors. Due to the great commercial potential connected to television rights, we have experienced a market in which the role of television broadcaster has become relevant also for other sectors. The entry of other players, active on the web through the offer of non-linear audiovisual service, is determining a new scenario where financial resources coming from advertising and subscriptions are shifting from traditional broadcasters towards the new media, mainly the OTT services. Moreover, OTT players are also beginning to produce their own programmes, and it is plausible that, in the next future, they will partially adopt a broadcaster business model integrated with the SVoD business model. The analysis developed in the chapter, with reference to traditional broadcasters, could fit partly to the emerging business model of OTT players.

DOI: 10.1057/9781137378477.0012

7.2 Broadcasters negotiating TV copyrights in the domestic market

Television broadcasters attain the availability of the products, which they insert in their programming, producing or buying them. Production and purchase are, generally, financed by personal resources coming, primarily, from advertising proceeds; from subscription taxes, in the case of public television or pay television; and from government transfers for public broadcasters.

The primary role taken on by television broadcasters in the audiovisual industry is born, above all, from the economic availability recorded in the phases of economic growth. The mechanism is easy to understand. The television channel broadcasts the programmes, the public follows them and the audience is the "merchandise" which advertising agencies negotiate. A programme which can gather a greater audience picks up more advertising and, consequently, being more attractive to advertising agents, has at its disposal a higher budget to be produced or purchased. Lastly, is the company that buys the advertising which finances the television product. The final consumer of the television product is represented by the advertising agent who in time has taken on the role of main funder. Such financial dynamics, typical of commercial television, are valid also for public broadcaster, which today can count on government funds less and less.

Since the gathering of television advertising depends on the ability of other businesses to invest in advertising, and this, in turn, depends on the macroeconomic cycle, generally, the financial availability of the broadcaster is greater in the phases of economic expansion, while it registers a reduction in the contraction phases of the economic cycle. The extensive economic cycles recorded in the 80s in developed countries, and lasting almost 30 years, have handed to television important financial resources from advertising. The other types of audiovisual firms have not been able to count on such significant financial resources, and this circumstance has made television broadcasters the strongest financial players on the market, and those apt to condition the production and the price of a great range of audiovisual products, even if not primarily related to television exploitation.

> The main financier of the television product is the firm which buys advertising; it represents the true price-maker of the market of television copyrights;

DOI: 10.1057/9781137378477.0012

production budgets and purchase prices of television products are, this way, strongly correlated to the macroeconomic cycle and to the financial availability of advertisers. This also affects production budget and price of cinema products.

To understand the financial dynamics of a television product – and somehow of cinema ones – we need, therefore, to understand the mechanism of emphasizing the value of the product in the eyes of firms which buy advertising time and understand how this mechanism could be coherent with editorial policies of broadcaster. To this objective, it is necessary to introduce the concept of television programme schedule. The understanding of such mechanism will be functional also in valuing products apt for other markets, like those in the cinema field, but we find in television copyrights the most important exploitation market.

Television product: value and programme schedule

The commercial potentialities of the television product contribute strongly to condition its value, may it be expressed in production costs or purchase price. Other than the artistic aspects of the product, the commercial potentialities depend also on the broadcaster's negotiation ability and, above all, on its editorial policies. The tool which translates in concrete terms the editorial policies of a television firm is the television programme schedule. The TV schedule is the tool through which television programming is accomplished, which has the aim to place the programmes in a specific temporal space for broadcasting. This fact is of fundamental importance in the value of a programme. The day and the viewing time during which the programme is broadcasted conditions the number of potential viewers and, therefore, it could make the product more or less attractive in the eyes of advertising agents.

The use of television by viewers is seasonally characterized, which determines audience figures at different times of the year, of the week, of the day. Since television consumption varies in time, and the different viewing times address a diverse number of viewers, and a different make up of it, the television firm has the objective of placing the programmes in more adequate time-bands according to programming policies. Considering programming, the year is divided in seasons (Fall-Winter, Spring and Summer), the week is divided among working days and holidays, the day in time-bands. In particular, a programming day is divided in three main time-bands: *day-time*, *prime-time* and *night-time*. *Day-time*

DOI: 10.1057/9781137378477.0012

corresponds to a time-band which goes from morning until night and, generally, it has an average audience level; *prime-time* is that of dinner time and is identified as the highest audience time-band, *night-time* is the night-band, which corresponds to reduced viewing figures.

The main aim of the television firm is to maximize the viewing figures on all time-bands, and in particular on *prime-time*. Public television and commercial television try to reach the aim of the viewing data having to associate it to different *missions* of the firm. Public television, for example, has to conciliate the aim of the audience figure with that of access, that is, the greatest use of television by all *target* viewers; commercial television, on the contrary, can reach the audience target concentrating only on specific segments of viewers. The more the broadcaster finances itself with advertising, the more it has the necessity to reassure to advertisers the level of *audience* guaranteed, and for which they have paid. Essentially, advertisers pay for advertising space in relation to the type of programme and the time-band of the programme itself; the price paid by the advertisers is valued according to the viewing figures foreseen. The television firm has to, therefore, try to reach the level of guaranteed *audience*, without falling too much below, but without going overboard to avoid free public contact. The number of viewers can be measured thanks to various variables:

a) *average viewing*, that is the average number of spectators present in a determined time interval;
b) *contact*, that is the number of times that the spectators have tuned in on a channel in a determined time space;
c) *share*, that is the percentage of spectators who are tuned on a single broadcasting in a determined time interval in relation to all the spectators who, at the same interval, are watching television.

Independently from the used calculation variable, it is always true that the advertising agent is willing to pay more for programmes which bring home the greatest audience. Therefore, the general rule at the base of TV programme schedule policies is that the cost of a programme should be adequate to the hosting time-band, and therefore, lastly, to the profits obtained from the selling of advertisement.

Theoretically, for commercial television, and in part also for public ones, since the programmes are financed by advertising, and advertisers pay according to viewing data, the programmes must cost considering the audience figures which presumably they can obtain.

DOI: 10.1057/9781137378477.0012

The cost of a television programme – whether it is a production cost or a purchase cost – has to consider the programming logic. Each segment of time has a different commercial value, and the profits are functions of the segment of time: it goes without saying that programming has to be based on a reliable estimation of foreseen audience figures and the cost of a programme has to be coherent with the time-band in which it will be placed.

The cost of a television product, expressed in terms of production costs or the purchase price, is correlated to its position in the programming. A different placing can bring about, for the same product, a different value.

> There is not a cost and a sole price of a television product, but a different cost and a different price considering the placing of the product within the schedule programmed by the television firm. The same product can be valued differently, either by the same firm or by different broadcaster, depending on the programming time-bands in which it is inserted.

This general rule is not, likewise, always pursuable; different variables exist which can determine variations of cost and of price from the average one of the programming time-band originally individualized.

First of all, we consider the efficiency in the make-up of the TV schedule. The broadcaster, indeed, tends to satisfy the advertising agent, counting, alternatively, to maximize the difference among revenues and costs, or to minimize the audience costs. The more the television firm is able to place a product in the viewing time-band which maximizes the difference between revenue and costs, or minimizes the audience cost, the more it will be able to profit on the product; alternatively, it could, using that profit, produce more expensive products, or acquire products at more expensive prices.

The efficiency in the build-up of the programme schedule allows, at even advertising revenues, to maximize margins or, alternatively, to have higher budgets for producing and purchasing the products.

The build-up of the TV programme schedule is, also, conditioned by the firm's internal and external variables; among the internal ones the image of the channel stands out (that is its stable style in time), the identity of the channel (represented by the type of audience it refers to) and the logical sequence of the schedule, according to which a programme cannot be placed in whatever time segment. Among the external ones, the demand of advertising spaces coming from advertisers becomes

DOI: 10.1057/9781137378477.0012

significant, the availability of the adequate product, the programming of competitors, the audience humour.

The result is that, taking into account the TV schedule, the value of a television product, in terms of production costs or of price, is influenced from (Figure 7.1):

a) *the availability of financial resources coming from advertising*: in times characterized by positive economic trends, the advertising gathering assures greater resources and television firms can opt for more expensive programmes; for this reason, it is easy to find higher production budgets and average purchase prices in expansive economic phases and lower budgets and average prices decreasing in receding economic phases;
b) *the necessity to satisfy the needs of advertising agents*: the restriction of having to assure to the advertiser the viewing result promised can lead to the need of having to produce or purchase, however, a specific product with the risk of having to provide high production

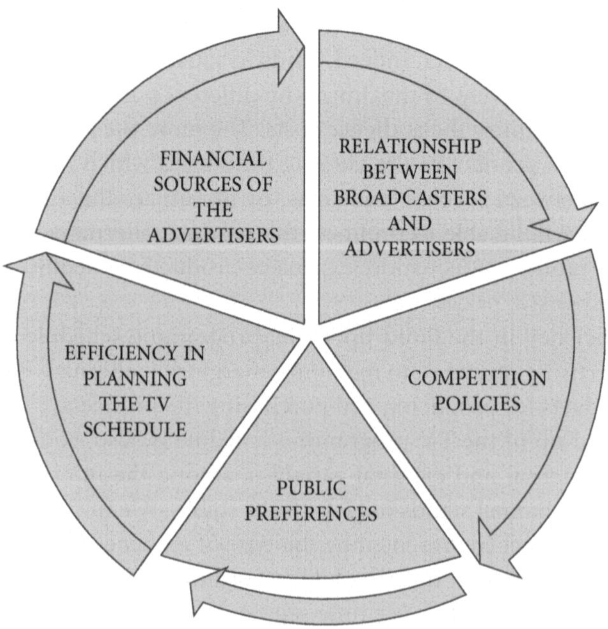

FIGURE 7.1 *TV schedule and determinants of value of TV products*

DOI: 10.1057/9781137378477.0012

budgets or high purchase prices, and of having to accept packaged purchases, which include other than sought-after products and also less attractive products;

c) *the necessity to answer to the programming of competitors*: having to face the editorial choices of competitors can create the need to carry out an aggressive programming – or an anti-programming – which can result in an increase of costs related to producing or buying well known products, able to contrast those shown by competitors, or to deprive competitors of the availability of certain programmes;

d) *the uncertainty related to the mood of the audience*: the necessity to obtain a positive audience answer can lead the television firm to allocate in different programming time-bands products of higher quality to that of the average of the group; it comes down to, that in some circumstances, the production and the purchase cost of the products is not proportioned in relation to the programming time-band in which it is inserted.

> The value of a television product is inspired to editorial programming, but it is conditioned by the efficiency in the build-up of the TV programme schedule, by the financial availability of advertisers, from the relationship of the broadcaster with the suppliers and from competitors' policies. The combined result of such variables do not allow the identification of a value, and so of a cost and of a price, for any single product, nor for the build-up of benchmark values of reference.

The logic of the build-up of the programme schedule, nevertheless, impugns the value for singular titles and moves the plan of valuing of the television product on a portfolio approach: or more than on the evaluation of the single product, the television firm operates a value of product pockets by audience time-grids, following a logic of cross-collateralization of revenues, according to which the lower revenues recorded on certain products and on specific audience time-bands are subsidized by the greater revenues obtained by other products on other programming bands.

> The modern logic of TV programme schedule moves towards the cross-collateralization of revenues and makes the identification of a value of a single title less significant; it becomes meaningless, however, also the definition of a benchmark value for homogeneous products, even when placed within the single programming bands.

DOI: 10.1057/9781137378477.0012

Business models and negotiation of TV rights

The negotiation of television copyrights within the domestic market takes on different characteristics and different signs in relation to the business model. When the television firm is also producer, the right of exploitation is already in its title. In this case, the negotiation happens between the broadcaster and advertising concessionaires and the broadcaster becomes the seller. This is so, naturally, even in the case of productions given under contract to small companies, because the broadcaster keeps the title of the copyright. In rare cases, some independent producers can find themselves in the position of producing autonomously fortunate TV series, or movies, which are the object of negotiation with national TV broadcasters. Only in this case, the right of exploitation is object of negotiation between the producer and the broadcaster, and it becomes the buyer. In this case, the value of such right is directly connected to programme schedule policies of the broadcaster, and to the product's success with its audience, but it is also strongly conditioned by the negotiating strength of the parts.

7.3 Broadcasters negotiating TV rights in the international market

The structure of the market for international sales: United States vs. Europe

On the foreign market, the negotiation of television copyrights exploitation becomes peculiar. To understand better the negotiation of television copyrights on international markets, it is necessary to start from the structure of the demand and of the supply in such markets. These can be classified in demand-driven and supply-driven markets.

For European producers, for example, the access of their product on the international market is a complex question. European products, generally, have a strong local artistic matrix and, often, are conditioned by the native language; they present, however, a reduced level of universality and a low potential of exportation. For this reason, with the due exceptions, the foreign market represents a minimum quota of proceeds of a European audiovisual product.

> The European market of television copyrights is substantially demand-driven; for European broadcasters, negotiations are mainly finalized to buying a foreign product, rather than selling a domestic product.

DOI: 10.1057/9781137378477.0012

On the contrary, the American audiovisual industry is among the few which registers high levels of exports of its own product. Even if, in time, the trend of foreign sales of American products has undergone diverse variations, it is possible to say that the American market is supply-driven.

> The American market of television copyrights is substantially supply-driven; for American broadcasters the negotiations are oriented primarily to the sales of national products.

The structure of the market allows identification of some characterizing elements of the international market of television copyrights. Traded products are primarily those of the fiction type, more apt to be exported and ready to meet the interest of viewers in diverse geographic areas. Since the market of copyrights referred to foreign products needs a specific knowledge of the foreign market, the commercial chain foresees, generally, the presence of third parties who mediate among producers and buyers.

Considering such scenery, the value of the product is essentially a value referred to the price of purchase; only in the case of international participation and co-productions, for the broadcaster the value of the product has also a dimension connected to the cost of production and to the sale price of the copyrights.

The price of the copyright, other than being affected by the contractual strength of the parts, and of the programming policy of the broadcaster, is strongly conditioned by the complex commercial chain and from a relevant degree of informative asymmetry among buyers and sellers.

The different nature of European and American markets has led to a different distributive structure of the same: the first integrated by television firms, the second by distribution firms.

Substantially, since American television firms do not buy in a significant way foreign products, in the United States the international television market is *sales-oriented*, so supported by the interest of producers to sell: are, than, the majors that, through their subsidiaries or through third-parties operators, try to place their products abroad.

In Europe, the international television market is purchase-oriented (*buy-oriented*), since television firms tend to get abundant foreign product to insert within their own channels.

The union of two markets with opposing needs (of sales the American one, of purchase the European one) and with differently integrated distributive structures (of production the American one, of distribution

DOI: 10.1057/9781137378477.0012

the European one) has determined a lengthy commercial chain which unwinds through more intermediaries and produces numerous negotiating steps.

Actors active in the market of international sales

The international market of television copyrights today is characterized by the existence of a compound commercial chain in which three categories of subjects operate: the production firms, the third-party operators that become intermediaries among producers and buyers and that can assume different roles and functions, and the television firms.

Producers are essentially represented by the so called "international majors", in particular the American ones, able to furnish continuously universal and spectacular product and content, so to have success at the international level, not only domestic. The role of independent producers is, on the contrary, classified as marginal and characterized by a sporadic presence attached to single products.

Among *third-party* subjects, it is possible to classify three categories of operators: the agents, the distributors and the intermediaries.

The agent represents the less structured figure; it identifies itself with a person, or a firm, that, stemming from a formal mandate of representation – or informally – functions as an intermediary between the production of which it takes care of the interests and a local broadcaster, probing and verifying the interest of the broadcaster to purchase specific products. The agent does not get involved in a sale contract, which is signed directly by the parties, and does not take on any risks or obligations. At the base of its mediation, the agent asks for a fee calculated as a percentage of the sale price. The business between the agent and the producer ends with the conclusion of the contract and the settlement of the agreed compensation.

The distributor is a specialized firm in the acquisition from the producer of the licencing copyrights of the work, for specific areas and for defined periods and in the exploitation of such copyrights. In the *distribution deal* the producer and the distributor define the characteristics of the deal and the role of distribution; the *sales agreement* establishes the terms of the deal between the distributor and the purchasing television broadcaster.

Generally, the financial role of the distributor is to cover the distribution expenses; sometimes, the distributor anticipates to the producer part of the future revenues assuring him a *minimum guarantee.*

DOI: 10.1057/9781137378477.0012

The possibility of a missed sale, or of a sale at a lower price from what expected, exposes the distributor to the risk of losing the expenses incurred, and of the *minimum guarantee*. Even the producer is exposed to the risk of not having any revenues from the sale, if the amount of the sale is not enough to cover what is due to the distributor to cover the expenses and as a distribution fee.

Summarizing, the distributor takes risks, but has a limited risk exposure; there is an economic and calculated connection which connects the producer and the distributor during the sale period; the distributor has to report to the producer a detailed account of revenues and their sharing.

The intermediary is represented by a firm, or more rarely by a person, who buys from the producer the copyrights of one or more products, for a specific time period and for specific areas. Substantially, we are facing a subject who assumes the property of the copyrights, making a purchase preceding a future sale (so it does not buy on commission), and takes on the risk of no sales, or the risk that what has been bought will not be "placed on the market"; the risk is that the purchased merchandise would remain "in stock". This role coincides with a pure intermediary figure defined "*dealer*", which in the audiovisual industry is known as "*entrepreneur*", to distinguish it from simple agents and from distributors. For the *entrepreneur*, however, the initial financial pledge coincides with the full price of transfer of the copyrights of exploitation and with the necessary expenses to sell the copyrights on foreign markets.

Generally, resorting to an intermediary is extremely useful because the intermediary who operates as *entrepreneur*, contrary to the agent and to the distributor, frees the majors of numerous operational, economic, financial and legal risks, by accepting them. In particular:

a) the *operational risk*, referring mainly to the predisposition and to the handing over of materials of the product sold apt to the needs of the buyer for the specific area, is transferred to the intermediary;
b) the *financial risk* is reduced because the sale to the intermediary happens in advance – often even before finding the effective final buyer, and often even before the product is made; the financial dynamics of payments of the majors are, so, attached to the relationship between major and intermediary, and only indirectly to those between intermediary and buyer;

DOI: 10.1057/9781137378477.0012

c) the *economic risk* of the sale, is cancelled because it is transferred to the intermediary;
d) the *currency risk* is void because transferred to the intermediary: between major and intermediary the contract is, however, always regulated in money of the major;
e) the *legal risk* is void because transferred to the intermediary who stipulates the contract with the buyer;
f) the *fiscal risk* – understood as possible application of taxes on revenues coming from the exploitation abroad of the copyrights – is void because transferred to the intermediary;
g) the monitoring of proceeds flow (*monetary risk*) is taken care of at a domestic level because it is referred only to dealing between major and the intermediary;
h) the book-keeping for a single title is negotiated with the intermediary (*allocation risk*).

Considering the risks, the intermediary is invested of a significant bargaining power in the negotiation with the broadcaster – resulting conditioned only for the duration of the availability of the right and the geographical areas where he can act – and he is independent from the major in defining the sale conditions to apply. The sale contract which the intermediary stipulates with the buying broadcaster is not governed by the producing major that supplies the product even if, unavoidably, it is affected by the financial-economic and contractual conditions existing between major and intermediary. Considering so, the potential profit of the intermediary does not foresee a "cap" from the original contract of purchase of the product and, theoretically, there are no limits, other than what can derive from the dynamics of the market. Therefore, in the market of television copyrights a final price imposed or suggested by the producer and the distributor is not recognized, as it is for some industrial products. The intermediary can act at his own discretion to set up the *mark-up* and the final price of a certain product and can at his own discretion differentiate it by areas. So it happens, then, that the same product could register different sale prices within different areas, either if such areas have as reference the same intermediary, or in the case – more obvious – in which different intermediaries take care of different areas.

> The intermediary who operates as entrepreneur takes care personally of the contract with the broadcaster and is not subject to any cap from the major on

DOI: 10.1057/9781137378477.0012

the final price that he could ask to the purchasing television broadcaster. The same intermediary is free to apply, for the same product, different prices to broadcasters operating in different countries.

What was said is true, specifically, for the intermediary *entrepreneur*, for the figure which corresponds to the *dealer* and that, not inverting the business cycle, takes on the financial and unsold warehouse risk. It can also happen that on the market are found intermediaries operating using an inversion of the business cycle that from "production-sale" transforms to "sale-production". It is always an *entrepreneur* who, but, in this case, buys from the major or from independent producers the rights of exploitation only when he has a specific request from a foreign broadcaster. This happens, in particular, when a request of specific products is put forward directly by the broadcaster, already a client of the intermediary. In such circumstances, the intermediary carries out a "short selling", that is the sale of a product not yet in stock. Normally, to manage the risk of a "short selling", the intermediary tends to combine as much as possible the timing of the sale contract with the purchase contract; it can happen, in such a scenario, that the two prices – of sale from the major to the intermediary and of purchase of the broadcaster from the intermediary – are contextually negotiated. Such circumstance can be found, above all, in contexts in which the relationship among intermediaries and clients has become solid in time, and in which the intermediary is not alone in proposing its own products in portfolio, but the client itself commissions some specific titles according to the needs matured within the firm. In such cases, either to safeguard the relationship with the intermediary, to avoid the dispersion of *shopping around*, or because, more often, it is a restricted number of titles, the broadcaster prefers however to resort to the intermediary, preferring him to the direct purchase from the major. It results in a dynamic of the make-up of the price more similar to the typical one of the agent.

Television firms active in different areas distinguish themselves for two essential variables: the technological paradigm, which determines the modality of broadcasting the programme, and the structure of the financing. In relation to the first aspect, it is possible to distinguish among cable, terrestrial, satellite and digital television; in relation to the economic criterion, we need to distinguish public firms and commercial television.

Each television firm, independently from its own nature and from broadcasting technologies, has the need to supply itself with products to

DOI: 10.1057/9781137378477.0012

place in its programming. However, the combination between economic and technological variables which characterize it conditions strongly the policies of *pricing*. There are three variables to point out:

a) *the degree of vertical integration of the firm*: this can cover all or part of the value chain of the sector, from the creation of content to production, from the multimedia packaging to the offer of extra services, until the distribution and the furnishing of the infrastructure for transmitting the signal;
b) *the level of multi-channels and the number of programmes*: television firms are different due to the number of channels and the number of programmes; the different modalities of broadcasting bring about various costs and allow different availability of channels;
c) *sources of funding*: public television finds its financing primarily in public funds and in subscription fees and, secondly, in commercials coming from private firms; commercial television has as its exclusive resource advertising; pay television is financed either by advertising or thanks to subscriptions.

It is understandable how the three variables strongly affect the *pricing* adopted by the firm. A greater degree of vertical integration makes the firm more autonomous from the purchase function and gives it a strong negotiating stance; a greater level of multi-channels and of programmes increases the need of the product and puts the firm in a weak condition in relation to the seller; the great or minor dependence from advertising resources connects the ability of purchase to the variance of the economic cycle: positive economic trends translate in a greater advertising gathering and increase the potentiality of expenditure, negative trends lessen the budget available for purchases.

Substantially, the characteristics of the television firm determine different needs of product, different bargaining strengths and different volumes of expenditure. The result is that, on the international television market, and within single countries, various firms can endure, for the same product, purchasing prices strongly differentiated, of which each one can be coherent with the organizational and economic structure of the firm itself.

> The structure of the television firm conditions the pricing of the product to be bought. When on the market there are firms with a different structure and a different volume of expenditure, there is neither a sole price for the same product, nor for homogeneous products, but each price has its own economic rationality.

DOI: 10.1057/9781137378477.0012

Typologies of deals and agreements for international sales

The negotiating mechanisms of television copyrights on international markets follow procedures which have consolidated themselves in time and have been dictated, mainly, by the distributive structure of markets oriented to sales and by markets oriented to purchasing, as to also by the specific needs of counter-parties.

It is clear how the different distributive structures generated by American producers, oriented to sales, have met up with those of European television, oriented to purchasing, and as to how such meeting has determined the consolidation of progressive negotiating *steps*, mediated by third-party intermediaries in relation to producers and buyers, with a consequent increase of the number of commercial steps.

In such a scenario, the true market presents a multitude of negotiating schemes which meet the different needs of sellers and buyers.

The objectives of seller and buyer are different in relation to three elements:

a) the *type* of product;
b) the *amount* of product;
c) the *conditions of exploitation* of the product: geographical area, period of exploitation, number of runs.

The producer wants to sell, together with a quality product, also the less successful product, to sell all the available product and to offer the least possible number of licenses and reruns. The buyer is interested in purchasing the best product, to get only the product which appeals to him and to obtain the greater number of licenses and reruns.

The necessity to conciliate the opposing needs of sellers and buyers makes it necessary to resort to different negotiating schemes in view of the alternative which best combines the needs of counter-parties. The presence of agents, distributors and intermediaries on the international sales market is principally justified by such necessity because in different hypotheses it corresponds to the best solution of negotiation.

Among the many alternatives, the most significant ones, and which are greatly relevant in this case, are connected to two specific negotiating options:

a) the *output* deal and the *volume deal* stipulated directly among majors and television broadcasters;
b) the *package deal* stipulated among intermediaries and broadcasters.

DOI: 10.1057/9781137378477.0012

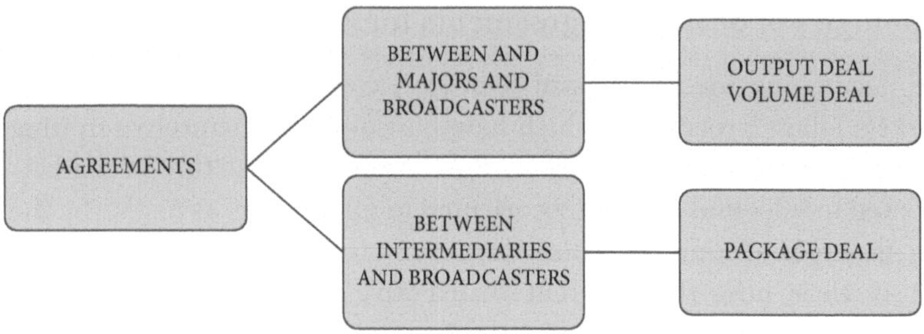

FIGURE 7.2 *Types of agreements for the sale of TV copyrights*

Generally television firms use both options, which can take on different meaning, due to the conditions of the market and the strategies adopted by the television firm (Figure 7.2).

Sales between majors and broadcasters: output deal and volume deal

The contracts stipulated by television firms directly with the majors have, generally, the objective of covering the structural needs of product of the firm. Substantially, the *broadcaster* looks, through a direct deal with the major, to assure itself a supply at the source. The *output deal*, in fact, establishes a pledge by the firm to buy, and an obligation by the major to sell, all the product created by the major in a determined period pointed out by contract; the *volume deal* circumscribes the same contractual object to a specific volume of product.

Such contracts have, generally, a multi-year duration, variable from 3 to 5 years, and include as a purchasing object an articulated mix of products which include the main types: *output deal* and *volume deal* include, always, both television and cinema products, of *current* type (never previously distributed within the area of purchase) and of the *re-run* type (already distributed on the territory). The contract includes also a precise outline of the qualifying elements of the product and the purchasing conditions; for example, for cinema products it is possible to establish what are to be bought by the *broadcaster*: one option is to select, among all the movies produced by the major, only those distributed during the year within the purchasing area; for *re-run* movies, can be fixed a maximum amount of a yearly purchase, with the *broadcaster* having the

DOI: 10.1057/9781137378477.0012

freedom of choosing the titles from the list of the major or, alternatively, can be fixed the number of titles to be bought and their unitary value. Also for television products, in the contract are specified both the quality standards of *re-run* products and those of *current* products; for the series, we can foresee integral purchase of the series, or the buying of episodes related to only one season, with the option of the purchase of the next season. Also for television products, the contract specifies, generally, the characteristics which they need to have; for example, for buying TV series it can be indicated as requirements of the product to be bought the value of the production budget or the number of series or the format.

With the agreements of *output deal* and *volume deal* the *broadcaster* has the benefit of assuring itself a significant quantity of product in comparison to a disadvantage represented by the uncertainty in relation to the product which it is obligated to buy. As a matter of fact, above all, from the second year on of the contract time, even if the qualifying elements of the product indicated in the contract limit the arbitrage of the supply, the television firm will find itself in the condition of selecting an unknown product because it has been produced at a time later than the signing of the contract.

Package deal

Thanks to *package deals* stipulated with intermediaries, television firms take care of the necessity of integrative and variable products. Substantially, once a minimum and generic stock of products has been reassured, the package deal allows broadcasters to meet: (a) related to quantity, the needs dictated by additional use to cover hours of programming; (b) related to quality, the necessity of having at one's disposal the single and specific products already known.

According to contracts among intermediaries and majors, intermediaries can think of putting together a *package deal*, pure or mixed. Generally, the intermediary stipulates a *package deal* with the television firm offering products already bought from the major, titles which he has already at his disposal (pure *package deal*). In some cases, the intermediary can integrate the offer with added titles not yet available at his disposal, requested directly from the *broadcaster*; this is common when the television firm does not have an *output* or *volume deal* with the major represented by the intermediary and expresses the need of product of the major not included in the original package of the intermediary and not

DOI: 10.1057/9781137378477.0012

at his disposal. In this case, the intermediary operates in a mixed way: as pure intermediary for titles which he has already in his portfolio and as a *broker* for the titles which he adds to the original packet, thanks to a specific input of the television firm, but that he will have to buy from the major. In this case, the intermediary limits his exposition to risk, both in relation to the risk of not sold and to the temporal *gap* between the buying of rights and the sale of the same.

Output/volume deal vs. package deal

The different intrinsic characteristics of the two typologies of agreement, those used to close the deal with the major producers and those used with intermediaries, determine an impact also on the average prices generally applied in contracts (Figure 7.3).

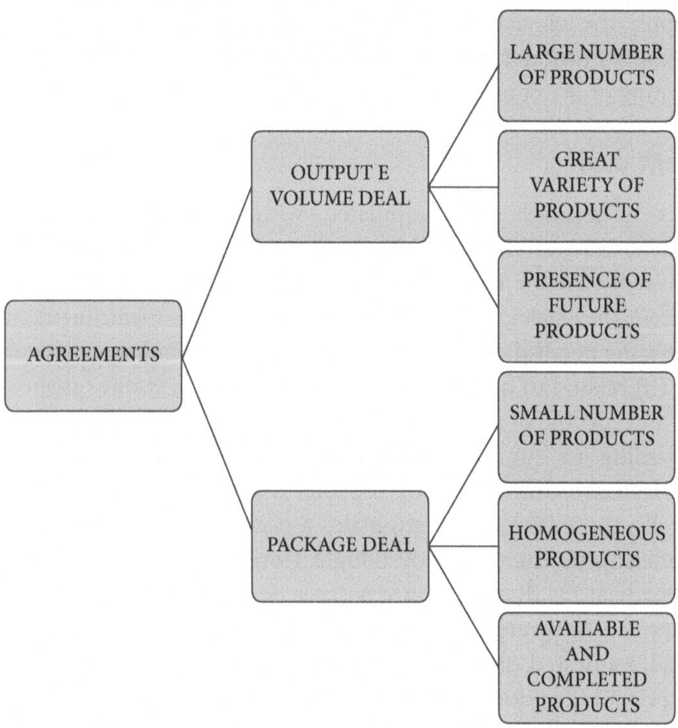

FIGURE 7.3 *Output and volume deal vs package deal*

DOI: 10.1057/9781137378477.0012

In relation to the *output deal* and to the *volume deal*, the *package deal* can be made up also by a limited number of titles (up to a minimum of two or three titles) and can relate only to specific typologies of product (cinema, television, *current* or *re-run)*: it results, however, strongly cut out on the specific needs of the *broadcaster.* Naturally, it is not a perfect tailored product because even the intermediary – who has bought or needs to buy from the major – is conditioned by the need of getting rid efficiently of his own portfolio titles, minimizing the risk of storage, that is, the risk of some unsold products. Excluding such consideration, is, however, without any doubt that the *package deal* represents a less standardized contract, in relation to the *output* and *volume deal*, thanks to which the *broadcaster* overcomes the uncertainty of the product present in great quantity contracts stipulated directly with the major. Even in relation to exploitation, there are differences between the two contractual typologies; *output deal*, *volume deal* and *package deal* foresee specific conditions of exploitation sufficiently standardized – for cinema products, generally, 5 passages in 5 years while for television series the conditions can be more favourable. However, often, in the *package deal*, the *broadcaster* is able to obtain exploitation conditions more convenient than those usually negotiated.

The different level of standardization of the purchased basket of products, and the highest level of risk incorporated in the *output and volume deal*, in relation to future products still unknown at the time of the contract, determines a first strong variation in the average level of price between the two types of agreement. Substantially, the contracts stipulated by television firms with the major foresee, generally, average purchase prices lower than those stipulated with the intermediaries. So apart from the mark-up applied by the intermediary. The two types of contracts put together, as a matter of fact, types of different products with different characteristics of the package and different disclosure of the product.

> Generally, the output and the volume deal are more convenient for the buying television firm in terms of the quantity of the product and of price; the package deals stipulated with the intermediary are more convenient in terms of product quality and of exploitation conditions. It is not, however, possible to compare, not even for the same type of products, the average price paid by a television firm for an output or volume deal with the price obtained on the package deals.

DOI: 10.1057/9781137378477.0012

The mechanisms of valuing of the products purchased, or through *output and volume deal* or in packets by intermediaries, introduce an additional critical element in comparing the price among various contracts.

The valuing of products happens through an *escalator* which applies different price levels in relation to the value of some economic variables referred to the product. For cinema products, the used parameter is the *box office*: the higher the *box office*, the higher the sale price. For television products, the more used reference parameter is the *hourly cost for format*; for each type of format, the higher the cost of production the higher the sale price.

So, the value of the escalators varies, first of all, in relation to the type of product because cinema and tv products are valued based on different parameters. Also for homogeneous products, it is possible to find different values: first of all, because the majors can adopt different value of the *escalator*; for example, two movies of two different majors which have obtained the same *box office* can be valued differently according to different reference *escalator* used by the majors. Secondly, because the conditions which influenced the class of attribute in which the product is placed can be different: for movies, for example, the dimension of the purchasing market is important (the greater is the number of viewers, greater, with the same conditions, is the value of the product); for television products, the operational efficiency of the major (the greater operational efficiency of the major, means less hourly cost of production, even to other conditions) and its commercial policies. Additionally, in the *output deal* and *volume deal* the valuing has to incorporate the risk taken on by the buyer in relation to the missing knowledge of the product due to a future production.

The mechanism of valuing of the product determines, therefore, a strong variability of prices also for products homogeneous in technical-productive characteristics.

> The mechanism of valuing of television products, and in particular the parameters of the escalator adopted by the majors, do not allow a comparison of price, not even among homogeneous products, and hinder the singling out of a reliable benchmark price.

Lastly, there is another variable able to impugn the valuing of a television product and, consequently, of the *mark-up* and the final price applied by intermediaries: the production model of the majors. These produce, primarily, resorting to forms of co-production with independent producers and taking on, often, also the role of national distributor. Attributing a definite value to a single product for foreign sales (*allocation*) can be conditioned by the convenience of the major to exploit the single product in view of the

DOI: 10.1057/9781137378477.0012

dynamics of profits sharing with the independent producer. So, it is reasonable to hypothesize that the major would be oriented to exploit more those titles for which the proceeds of foreign sales do not have to be shared out with the independent producer. When such titles are not of great success or of great additional value, the resulting consequence is that the best products can be *valued at discount* and those of less success can be *valued at premium*. This attitude of the majors may determine several effects on the *pricing*:

a) in the agreements stipulated directly between the major and the television firm, an evaluating opacity is expressed by the single title which takes on a value not easily understandable;
b) the autonomy of television broadcaster, and of the intermediaries, in valuing every single product of the sold package, can be limited, at the source, by this specific need of the major;
c) in the agreements stipulated through intermediaries, a definite break in the economic link between the two prices can be caused: that of purchase by the intermediary from the major and that of sale by the intermediary to the television firm. If the major sells to the intermediary a quality product, giving it a low value, and the intermediary, in the sale to the television firm, applies a more coherent value, it can be determined a significant distance between the two prices that, yet, does not correspond to the economic substance of the transaction, but it is only the function of an accounting criterion used in valuing the product.

> The production model of the majors hit the value of the single title; the necessity to manage the allocation in function of the revenue sharing with associated producers determines a substantial impossibility to precisely reconstruct the value attributable to the single product. In sales channelled through intermediaries, such circumstance makes not significant the difference between the purchase price paid by the intermediary to the major and the sale price paid by the television firm to the intermediary.

7.4 The economic reasons for using intermediaries in international television markets

The presence of a long commercial chain in the market of international sales creates a different negotiation model from that used for domestic markets. In particular, the presence of intermediaries, including an extra commercial passage in relation to the direct negotiation between

DOI: 10.1057/9781137378477.0012

producer and broadcaster that buys the copyrights, influences the dynamics of pricing and those of the final price of the purchased product. The presence of intermediaries, other than finding justification in the services offered to selling majors and to televisions that buy, can be justified by an economic space that makes the negotiation triangularly convenient to all parties: majors, intermediaries and broadcasters. To verify the existence of such economic space, we need to recall what has already been explained in the matter of economics and of pricing and apply it to the negotiating schemes of international sales.

Economics and pricing of majors

The economics of the majors correspond to those of other producers of audiovisual works, also being characterized by the complexity of the business structure and by significant volume of production.

For the majors, the greatest difficulty in determining the pricing is that related to the estimation of revenues. If considering costs, the majors can operate looking for a greater operational efficiency which consents to knock prices down; from the revenues side, each valid alternative to limit the variability becomes the element of fundamental importance.

Resorting to intermediaries allows the majors both to cut down costs and to stabilize revenues; this allows them to apply to the intermediary, considering such advantages, reduced prices.

The Formula 5.4, which is significant of the pricing of a product, can be best expressed, in relation to the majors, as (Formula 7.1):

$$\text{sales revenues } (p \times q) = oc + dc + fc + ic + comr + techr + legr + unsr + \text{mark-up} \qquad 7.1$$

where:

p = price
q = quantity
oc = overhead costs
dc = direct costs of production
fc = financial costs
ic = insurance costs
comr = completion risk
techr = technical risk
legr = legal risks
unsr = unsold or stock risk

DOI: 10.1057/9781137378477.0012

The overhead costs of the majors refer to the cost of employees and to the general expenses; to these are added the direct expenses of single productions; the financial expenses are connected to the financial costs of the debts and to insurance costs. The risks refer to, primarily, to those of process or of completion (that is of no completion of the work or of the realization of a final product not corresponding to the projected prototype); to technical risks, connected to the quality of materials; to legal risks; and to the unsold risk (or unsold stock risk).

The major is interested in reaching and establishing the rate of programmed profit and, to reach such an objective, can follow four ways: increase the volume of sales, fix a higher unit price, cut down costs and limit the risk exposure. The major, however, will be interested to avail itself of an intermediary if such solution allows it to meet at least one of the conditions outlined.

Considering costs, as explained, resorting to the intermediary who functions as entrepreneur allows the major to cut down the burden connected to risks – except the completion one – and to some management costs. Considering revenues, for the major, the intermediary can be functional in stabilizing or in increasing the volume of sales: (a) closing contracts for more areas; (b) reducing the volume of the unsold of various areas.

The possibility to increase through the intermediary the number of areas and to minimize the percentage of the unsold makes it convenient for the major to close the negotiation with the intermediary even at lower prices of its own *technical price*, because the quantity of the sold product allows, just the same, the reaching of the desired *mark-up*.

Saving on costs, or stabilizing or increasing revenues, allows the major to apply to the intermediary reduced prices keeping unchanged its own rate of profit expected by the investment.

A simple example helps to quantify what is expressed above. Let us assume that, using the Formula 7.1, a major would be in the position of choosing between two alternatives available for the sale of two movies: that of the direct sale to the broadcaster and that of the sale through the intermediary. Let us assume that the economics of the pricing have been estimated, for each movie, in the amount of $5 for each typology of cost and of risk, for a total of $40 for each movie, and that the mark-up wanted for each movie is equivalent to $10 (25%) for a total of $20 on two movies[1]:

DOI: 10.1057/9781137378477.0012

I. Direct sale

In the hypothesis of direct sale, the Formula 7.1 of the pricing would be equal to:

$$50 \text{ x } 2 = 10 + 10 + 10 + 10 + 10 + 10 + 10 + 10 + 20 \qquad 7.2$$

The unit price for each movie which assures the programmed profit rate should be equal to $50.

II. Sale with intermediary

Let us assume that resorting to an intermediary translates in a saving, for each one of the two movies, of $1 on overhead costs, on financial costs and on legal costs, and to an annulment of technical and unsold risks, for a total saving of $16 on two movies. The pricing formula would signify a different equilibrium among revenues and costs:

$$37 \text{ x } 2 = 8 + 10 + 8 + 10 + 10 + 8 + 20 \qquad 7.3$$

The unit price which the major could apply to the intermediary on a single movie, leaving unchanged its own profit, would be equal to $37, $13 less of the applicable in the hypothesis of direct sale.

> Resorting to the intermediary, creates for the major an economic space for the application of lower unit prices in relation to the applicable price in the direct sale; selling to the intermediary, the major can apply prices below the price that it should attribute in the direct sale to reach the same rate of return.

Economics and pricing of intermediaries

Generally speaking, the economics of the pricing of an intermediary correspond to that of any other provider of services. The activity of intermediation is looked at as a service that, generally, is produced following the purchase, represents intangible goods, presents significant fixed costs whose level varies according to the nature of the activity of intermediation and offers – stand-alone – low economies of scale.

The difficulty in determining the *technical price* makes revenues an even more significant variable in the process of pricing. In relation to the economics, the intermediaries are naturally prone to focus their attention on the estimated revenues, rather than on a more efficient and accurate analysis of costs. Since, generally, the services are first sold and then produced, the intermediary has the possibility to estimate revenues with greater accuracy.

DOI: 10.1057/9781137378477.0012

Additionally, the activity of intermediation is characterized by a demand inelastic to prices: clients tend not to react to price changes or, alternatively, apply minimum changes on the quantity requested; rarely, facing a price variation, clients are inclined to change the furnishing firm.

On the contrary, the client pays attention to the perceived value, valuing on one hand, his need and the investment quality, on the other hand, the savings in terms of non-monetary costs which the work of the intermediary brings about. Also for this reason, the price of competitors loses part of its strength.

Such circumstances permit, generally, to the intermediary more possibilities to apply high mark-up and final prices, without incurring in a decrease of purchasing orders or losing the client.

For such reason, the pricing of the intermediation activity adopts less to a "cost-based methodology", and it is strongly conditioned by the orientation to maximize revenues. It is important, therefore, to understand what is the economic space to the pricing policy of the intermediary.

For an intermediary negotiating television copyrights the Formula 7.1 related to the pricing of the product takes on a different configuration (Formula 7.4) in relation to the one of the producing major; for the intermediary, the costs of completion are not present anymore, while the direct costs are connected to the purchase of product by the majors and are, consequently, comparable to the cost of raw materials of production of a traditional industrial firm:

$$\text{sales revenues } (p \times q) = oc + dc + fc + ic + techr + legr + unsr + \text{mark-up} \qquad 7.4$$

Also for the intermediary, as for the major, the objective is to maximize profit. However, compared to the major, the intermediary has a more rigid and less foreseeable structure. In terms of strictness of costs, contrary to the major, the possibility to outsource specific functions is very limited, because the intermediary represents himself as the commercial link with the buying broadcaster. In particular, technical, legal and unsold risks can take on *ex post* values much more important than those hypothesized. It is sufficient to think about the *unsold risk*: the cost of the unsold product can determine heavy loss on single negotiations. When the *unsold risk* is managed the intermediary has also borne a financial risk explained by the temporal gap elapsed between the buying date of the copyright by the major and that of sale to the broadcaster.

DOI: 10.1057/9781137378477.0012

Considering costs and risks, therefore, the intermediary can only activate the lever of his own managerial efficiency that, however, is limited by the difficulty, typical of services, in obtaining significant economies of scale.

Therefore, the intermediary uses the revenues as a main lever of his own pricing. Since the revenues depend on the price and on the quantity sold, he will try to sell more or at a higher price. The uncertainty about the level of costs and of risks translates itself, however, in the necessity to apply high mark-up, which affects the price, to obtain the margins of profit desired. The economic space produced by the negotiation with the major, therefore, makes it easy to apply a price compatible with the needs of the intermediary.

Let us look again at the example of the two movies bought by an intermediary at $37 each; let us assume that, for the sale of the movies to the broadcaster, the costs which the intermediary faces are the same of the half of those incurred by the major, that the intermediary attributes *the unsold risk* of the specific negotiation related to the two movies a quota part of his general risk of unsold goods equal to $5, and that the profit rate desired is the same of that applied by the major, therefore the 25% corresponding to almost $17 of mark-up per movie. We would have:

$$69 \times 2 = 5 + 74 + 5 + 5 + 5 + 5 + 5 + 34 \quad 7.5$$

The intermediary, to get the unitary rate of profit desired ($17) would need to apply a price equivalent to $69 per movie; this way he would obtain almost a yield of 25%. In relation to the purchase price of the major, equivalent to $37, the intermediary would apply an increase of almost 86% – that however would result equivalent to 38%, if compared with the price of $50 that the major would apply to the broadcaster in the case of direct sale.

In case the intermediary perceived the uncertainty of high costs and risks, his pricing should incorporate such prevision. Let us assume that the intermediary estimates it probable that one of the two movies of the bought package from the major is unsold; the pricing formula of the only sold movie, incorporating such risk, should however include the purchase cost of the unsold movie, and should cut down the value of costs from technical and legal risks not met because of the no sale, other than the mark-up on the second movie. So we would have:

$$116 \times 1 = 5 + 37 + 5 + 5 + 2.5 + 2.5 + (5 + 37) + 17 \quad 7.6$$

DOI: 10.1057/9781137378477.0012

If the intermediary would want to insure himself against the risk of one unsold movie, keeping his mark-up on the sold movie unaltered, he should sell the movie at the price of $116, with an increase of over 300% in relation to the purchase price, and of almost 230% in relation to the price that the major would apply to a direct sale to the broadcaster.

When the intermediary operates on an inverted cycle, the dynamics of pricing do not change in their basic structure: the *unsold risk* transforms in supplies risk, the financial risk is limited but, in the majority of cases, continues to be so.

Valuing the advantage of using intermediaries

The existence of an economic space that justifies the presence of an intermediary, therefore, needs to be verified, first of all, valuing the determinants of risks and costs incurred by the intermediary, secondly considering as a parameter the gap between the price applied by the intermediary to the broadcaster and the hypothetic *target price* applied by the major in the direct sale, and not comparing the sale price of the intermediary with that of the purchase from the major.

The gap between the purchase price of the intermediary from the major and the sale price to the broadcaster is not representative of the increase of cost taken on by the broadcaster, and consequently the burden to resort to the intermediary; a more correct estimate could be made comparing the price set by the intermediary with the hypothetic *target price* that the major would have applied to the broadcaster through a direct sale.

However, even the comparison between the price applied by the intermediary to the broadcaster and that applied by the major through direct sale, for how right it is in an optic of accounting methodology of pricing, is however impugned by the various negotiating and contractual structures and by the different mix of the products sold in the schemes of direct sales and in those through intermediaries.

7.5 The financial model inside the film market

It has been clarified that available funding sources to the film industry come from soft money and pre-sale of copyrights. With the only exception of the USA, the access to private funds is residual and represents a modest amount of the total budget (Figure 7.4).

DOI: 10.1057/9781137378477.0012

Public funding

Culture is one of the cornerstones of European policies; public aids to the audiovisual industry are allowed and designed as part of the internal and external policies of the European Union aimed at implementing the 2005 UNESCO Convention[2].

Due to the recognized cultural role of the audiovisual industry, every European country has gradually adopted various means of public support. In Europe, public aids are historically cinema-oriented; nevertheless, the digital revolution fostering the co-existence of traditional linear media and new digital and non-linear services has gradually extended the sphere of action of public supports to all cultural audiovisual products.

At a European level, the legal framework for public financing is represented by the *Cinema Communication*[3] and the *Creative Europe Programme*, which provides the "sub-programme MEDIA" dedicated to the audiovisual industry[4]. The rationality behind the financial supports to cultural sectors is that the culture is a key tool to promote the European single market and to foster social integration through the respect of cultural diversity. The so called "cultural exception" allows member States to grant support to the industry in accordance with the commitment of not distorting competition. In this respect, European and national public funds are intended primarily for small companies – mainly of the cinema sector – with low market share and independent from broadcasters, which are assumed not in need of public support and not always oriented at cultural products. Besides, aids to the audiovisual industry are allowed in accordance with the EU State aid regulation that sets limits to public support calculated in percentage of the product total budget: the greater the degree of cultural-

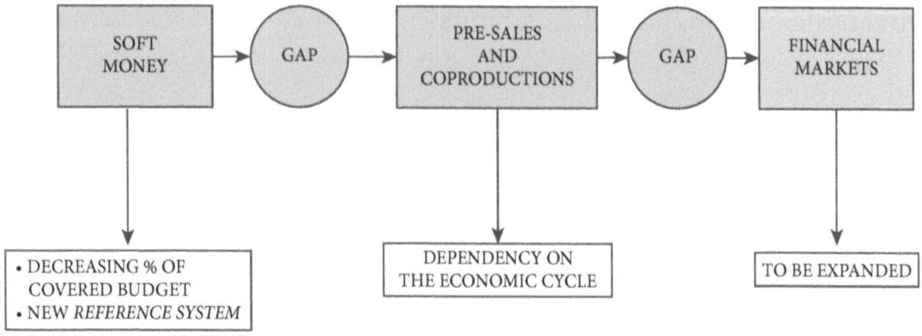

FIGURE 7.4 *Funding cycle of cinema firms*

DOI: 10.1057/9781137378477.0012

ity of the product supported, the higher the percentage of the budget that can be financed by national public funds.

At a country level, Governmental aids for the audiovisual business consist of national and local (regions, counties, councils) support. The national support, which involves the all production chains of the audiovisual industry – development, production, distribution, exhibition – is intended for the products, and funds are channelled through grants, soft financing or tax incentives, and can be issued automatically or through selective screening, based on specific reference systems. Local aids are mainly conceived to support producers and exhibitors, principally through the refurbishing/conversion of cinemas.

Public funding to the cinema sector has played in the last years a role always more marginal in quantitative terms. The percentage quota covering the budget by public funds has decreased gradually in time, considering the financial crisis and the decreasing public resources allocated to cultural sectors. Only short and documentary films, in relation to the degree of culturality and the recognized difficulty in tracing funds on the market, are mainly financed by public funds.

In a modern context, however, the importance of public funds in the financial cycle of the cinema industry is of a qualitative type. On one hand, public involvement has the task of indicating the cultural value of the product; on the other hand, it has the unquestionable function of being the strength of initiating the process of funding. This is explained by the fact that public funds are requested directly by the producer, without resorting to a distribution firm, already in the development phase and, therefore, represent, often, the first timely financing.

Pre-sale of copyrights

The movie industry is the most evident example of a financial model based on the discounting of future revenues. In quantitative terms, as a matter of fact, the financing of a movie product is mainly met by the pre-sale of copyrights. From a financial point of view, the movie industry is characterized by a significant mismatching between inflows and outflows; the proceeds, as a matter of fact, begin to translate into money only some months after the end of the production, with theatrical copyrights, while the revenues resulting from the other copyright markets can be obtained even after years from the *premiere* of the product. For such reason, the mechanism of pre-sales which allows a partial anticipa-

DOI: 10.1057/9781137378477.0012

tion of the revenues of future copyrights transfer, is fundamental in the financial equilibrium of cinema production firms.

The market of television copyrights represents one of the most important sources of the financing of cinema products. Until the 70s, the greatest source of revenues for the cinema coincided with the *box office* and the producer financed the movie asking for an advance on future theatrical proceeds. Afterwards, a decrease in movie-goers and an increase in television viewers have made television extremely important, both in an economic optic and the financial one.

Either in the case in which the producer makes a co-production with the broadcaster or in the case in which he produces autonomously, a significant part of financial funds necessary to produce the movie comes from the television firm which finances the work by pre-buying television copyrights. In such circumstances, the amount deriving from the pre-sale of the *cable-rights* corresponds, for the independent producer, to a revenue, and to a financing source.

In Europe, the importance of television broadcasters in the financing of the cinema sector is, therefore, stressed also by specific regulation: having to consider minimum percentages of programming of national and European movies, television broadcasters are indirectly subject to an obligation to invest a percentage of their own resources in cinema products. Such rules create another connection between the financial model of broadcasters and that of movie producers.

Generally, when the broadcaster participates in the project as a co-producer, television copyrights are negotiated in the co-production agreement directly between the broadcaster and the movie co-producer.

When the film company produces autonomously, the sale of television copyrights of the movie are often carried out by a distribution firm which takes care of the sale of the movie copyrights on all potential markets of exploitation. Even if the producer could negotiate autonomously his own copyrights, by praxis he relies on a distribution firm or, alternatively, can combine the two options. The distributor, other than taking care of the promotion and of the launching of the film, takes on, therefore, a decisive role for the economic exploitation of the work closing, for the producer, sale deals of copyrights on different channels of exploitation, domestic and international. In the cinema market, the distributor, generally, assures the producer an advance on future revenues – so called "minimum guarantee" – which he recovers primarily as the proceeds show in money. In such case, the distributor takes on

DOI: 10.1057/9781137378477.0012

the role of the leading external funder of the movie. Considering such service, the distributor asks for a commission and an absolute priority in the distribution of revenues up to a concurrence of the applied commission, of the expenses incurred for the distribution and the launch, of the amounts lent under a *minimum guarantee* title; only after the distributor has recovered these amounts, the revenues of the movie could be shared between the producer and the distributor himself.

To fully understand the financial model of the cinema industry it is necessary, therefore, to understand in detail the types of agreements generally used among producers and distributors.

More specifically, film production financial plans normally include recoupment agreements between producers and distributors: the so called "*distribution deal*".

The understanding of the recoupment agreement stated in the *distribution deal* is an essential requirement for a first evaluation of the reliability of the producer/distributor.

Typologies of distribution deals

There are two standard types of distribution contracts: *gross deal* and *net deal*.

In the *gross deal contract*, proceeds originating from the exploitation of a film are divided between producer (licensor of the rights) and distributor (licensee), according to certain percentages defined in the contract. The distribution company, due to the financial support provided for production, recovers its expenses according to such percentage.

The producer and the distributor will register a profit only in the case in which competency revenues, divided according to what stated in the distribution contract, will be above the costs incurred.

In the *net deal*, more commonly used, the revenues are allotted, first of all, to cover the anticipated expenses by the distribution (*minimum guarantee*, launch and edition expenses) and, only the remaining amounts are divided between producer and distributor according to the percentages established. Since the proceeds of the theatrical are not always sufficient to cover the expenses anticipated by the distribution, the net deal foresees, generally, a clause of cross-collateralization that acknowledges the possibility of using the revenues from the exploitation markets following the theatrical to reintegrate the distributor of the incurred costs. Such type of agreement states that the incurred expenses by the distribution (*minimum*

DOI: 10.1057/9781137378477.0012

guarantee and expenses of launch and edition) could be considered as advances granted to the production and, so, represent credits which the distribution has towards the producer. Such credits will be consequently reimbursed, having priority on revenues generated by the film.

The net deal foresees always the definition of one specific mechanism of revenue sharing between the producer and the distributor. Even if by praxis each agreement can have different characteristics in relation to the specific needs of the parts, and to the peculiar nature of the project, it is possible to trace two types of revenue sharing methodologies: lump sum (*cost off the top*) and dynamic (*pure net deal*).

The costs coverage and the subsequent revenues sharing between producer and distributor are carried out differently depending on whether the *cost off the top* method, rather than the *pure net deal* is used:

- the *cost-off the top* says that the revenues are destined, primarily, to cover distribution expenses and the minimum guarantee; only after are the revenues divided between producer and distributor based on the percentages established;
- the *pure net deal* says that the distributor keeps, from the first revenues, a distribution fee established by contract; the next revenues are destined primarily to cover distribution expenses – relying only on the producer quota – and only after are they divided between producer and distributor based on the percentages set by contract.

An example of net deal agreement

An example of a scheme of *net deal* helps to understand better the forms of revenue sharing between distributor and producer. The following example refers to an *art house film*, with a reduced budget, which has a significant *box office* and that offers the opportunity of exploiting copyrights even on markets post-theatrical.

Supposing (Table 7.1), that the movie in question has a production cost of €550,000. Supposing, moreover, that in the distribution agreement would be established a *minimum guarantee*, in favour of the producer, equivalent to €100,000 and that distribution expenses result equivalent to €200,000.

Suppose, then, that following the release, and considering the agreements of pre-sale, the revenues from the various markets are equivalent to €250,000 per *box office* (considered already net from the percentage

DOI: 10.1057/9781137378477.0012

TABLE 7.1 *An example of net deal: the assumptions*

COSTS	PRODUCER OUTFLOWS	DISTRIBUTOR OUTFLOWS	MARKETS OF EXPLOITATION	% REVENUE SHARING
550,000 PRODUCTION COSTS	450,000 (550,000–100,000 minimum guarantee)	200,000	THEATRICAL	70
200,000 DISTRIBUTION COSTS		100,000 MINIMUM GUARANTEE	HOME VIDEO	70
30% DISTRIBUTION FEE (only pure net deal)			PAY TV	70
			FREE TV	70

DOI: 10.1057/9781137378477.0012

detracted by exhibitors), €50,000 for Home Video, €100,000 for Pay TV and €150,000 for Free TV.

Suppose, lastly, that in the agreement would be established a revenues sharing mechanism, imagining that such distribution gives the producer 70% of revenues resulting from the exploitation of copyrights on various markets (theatrical, home video, Pay TV and Free TV), and to the distributor the remaining 30%.

In the hypothesis that the distribution contract followed the scheme of the *cost off the top* (Table 7.2), considering the cross-collateralization mechanism, the proceeds from *box office* and of Home Video are entirely destined to cover the anticipated expenses by the distribution (distribution expenses plus *minimum guarantee* assured to the producer). Only for revenues from the sale of copyrights to television follows the distribution between producer and distributor, according to the quotas established in the distribution agreement.

In the example given, then, the distributor recovers the anticipated expenses (€300,000) and obtains a profit equivalent to €75,000, while the producer registers a loss equivalent to €275,000, that is the net amount between the total production costs (€550,000) and the proceeds that, according to the agreements, has been able to use to cover such costs (€100,000 from *box office* and home video, to cover the *minimum guarantee* advanced by the distributor, and €175,000 from television sales to cover other production expenses incurred). In such case, the producer could reach the covering of expenses, and eventually get a profit, only through access to other exploitation markets of copyrights, or through

TABLE 7.2 *Cost off the top revenues sharing*

REVENUES	AGGREGATED REVENUE WATERFALS	PRODUCER SHARE 70%	DISTRIBUTOR SHARE 30%
THEATRICAL: 250,000	250,000	-----	------
HOME VIDEO: 50,000	300,000	------	------
RECOVERY OF DISTRIBUTION COSTS + MINIMUM GUARANTEE	300,000	------	------
PAY TV: 100,000	400,000	70,000	30,000
FREE TV: 150,000	550,000	105,000	45,000
TOTAL: THEATRICAL + FIRST SALES	550,000	175,000	75,000 (profit)

DOI: 10.1057/9781137378477.0012

copyrights sales on foreign markets, or still through second sales of copyrights on the national market.

Following a dynamic schema, typical of the *pure net deal*, generally used, the revenue sharing is more complex. First of all, as said before, the methodology includes always a commission on distribution – calculated on theatrical revenues – to cover the quota share of indirect structural costs of the distribution firm attributable to the specific project, and not included among the costs of edition and launch.

In such a scheme, then, the revenues resulting from the various forms of copyrights exploitation are distributed only theoretically according to the percent quotas set in the distribution agreement. Such distribution does not coincide with the true economic availability of the producer and of the distributor of their due sums. As a matter of fact, the priority of covering the anticipated expenses by distribution (distribution costs plus *minimum guarantee*) is met, initially, weighing on only the quota belonging to the producer. Only in the hypothesis when the producer quotas, related to the various exploitation markets, and accumulated, are not sufficient to cover the anticipated expenses, the coverage would be met also weighing on the quota nominally belonging to the distributor.

In the *pure net deal*, as shown by the example, a quota of the theatrical revenues is destined, first of all, to cover the distribution fee (Table 7.3). Once the distribution fee is subtracted, the producer quotas connected to the *box office* revenues (net from the distribution fee), to copyrights sales of home video, of Pay TV and of Free TV are destined, following the agreement and considering the mechanism of cross-collateralization, to cover the *minimum guarantee* and the distribution expenses. In the example given, from this project the distributor gets a net profit of €143,500, while the producer registers a loss equivalent to €418,000, that is at the net balance between the total cost of production (€550,000) and the revenues that, according to the agreement, have been destined to cover production costs (€100,000 to cover the *minimum guarantee* anticipated by the distributor, and €32,000 from the transfer of copyrights to Free TV to be used to cover the other production costs).

Also in such case, the producer will be able to reach costs coverage, and eventually obtain profits, only through access to other markets of copyrights exploitation, or through the sale of copyright on foreign markets, or through second copyrights sales on the national market. In

DOI: 10.1057/9781137378477.0012

TABLE 7.3 *Pure net deal revenues sharing*

REVENUES	AGGREGATED REVENUE WATERFALLS	PRODUCER SHARE	FEE (30%)	DISTRIBUTOR RECOVERING ON PRODUCER SHARE	DISTRIBUTOR SHARE
THEATRICAL: 250,000	250,000		75,000		
THEATRICAL (net of distribution fee): 175,000	250,000	-------		122,500	52,500
HOME VIDEO: 50,000	300,000			35,000	15,000
PAY TV: 100,000	400,000			70,000	30,000
FREE TV: 150,000	550,000	32,000		72,500 (out of 105,000)	45,000
RECOVERY OF DISTRIBUTION COSTS + MINIMUM GUARANTEE				300,000	
TOTAL: THEATRICAL + FIRST SALES	550,000	32,000		----------	142,500

DOI: 10.1057/9781137378477.0012

the *pure net deal* method, therefore, the distributor recovers his expenses weighing, first of all, on producer quotas: using distributor quotas to cover distribution expenses is residual and eventual; in the *cost off the top*, the producer and distributor quotas are added to reach the objective of covering costs: the distributor participates with his own quotas to cover the expenses incurred.

Whatever might be the performance of the product on various markets, in the distributor view the *pure net deal* is always more convenient; for the producer, on the contrary, the *cost off the top* represents the most advantageous way of distribution of revenues because it allows speeding up the recovery of expenses.

In reference to the revenues sharing, it is easy to notice how the dynamics of theatrical strongly influence the mechanism: with highly successful *box office* products the producer will regain possession of his own quotas of revenues more rapidly, according to the percentages established by contract, whether is used the *cost off the top* or the *pure net deal*.

The example illustrates a case which, in spite of a fair *box office* success, the total accumulated revenues generated by the theatrical and by first sales (€550,000) do not cover the total cost of production and distribution (€750,000) while they cover, nominally, all the costs of production (€550,000). It is easy to see, however, how applying the *cost off the top* and *the pure net deal*, the producer does not recover the expenses incurred. The distributor registers, in both cases, a profit, that, therefore, is more meaningful in the case of *pure net deal*.

The recoupment mechanisms included in distribution deals conventionally used determine, therefore, a mechanism of revenues sharing which assures a faster reaching of the economic equilibrium by the distributor. The producer's ability to increase profits depends, firstly, on the performance generated by the product at the theatrical level and is, then, strictly correlated with the artistic strategy adopted. Such contractual strength linked to the distributor finds its own ratio in the ability of the distributor himself to assure, at the same time, money for the production expenses and the closing of the circuit of the copyrights exploitation chain, and takes for granted the possibility that the producer could exploit the same copyrights on others and on different geographical markets. The choice between *net deal* and *gross deal*, between *cost off the top* and *pure net deal*, the same as the setting of percentages of the

DOI: 10.1057/9781137378477.0012

producer and distributor quotas depend, mainly, on the amount of the *minimum guarantee* assured to the producer and on the market power which the distributor can claim in assuring a profitable negotiation of the copyrights of the work. In synthesis, the distributor, on one hand is he who guarantees access to exploitation markets, and on the other hand takes on the role of a traditional financier, assuring a *minimum guarantee*; for such reasons, he has priority on waterfalls of revenues of the movie which allows him to reach an economic equilibrium more comfortably and more rapidly. For the producer, the cost of the distributor involvement is not sustained by an interest payment, as it would happen in case of a traditional financing, but in access to revenues conditioned by the main fulfilment of the distributor.

The types of agreement among producers and distributors bring out clearly how the financial model of the movie industry is strongly based on prospective proceeds. The presence of external financing is substantially absent and, in fact, substituted by a particular role taken on by distribution firms. Due to the financial crisis, the market is increasingly experiencing distribution deals with no minimum guarantee provided by distributors. This results in a more convenient revenue sharing mechanism for producers, who in contrast have to face a shortage of internal financial resourcers.

7.6 The financial model of the audiovisual web market

The economics at the base of the production process of web native audiovisual products, strongly conditions also the financial model.

The production dynamic of web products, centred on the self-reference of filmmakers, does not generate the urgency to implement sophisticated financial models. The costs, generally met by the same filmmakers, are designed on real resources of the authors; the amateurish nature of the product does not aim at looking for revenue sources on exploitation markets. Not foreseeing external financing in the production process, the objective to obtain revenues, therefore, is not even important to honour eventual debts towards third-party counterparts.

The outlined elements are characteristic of the audiovisual web native products promoted by filmmakers and small production companies.

DOI: 10.1057/9781137378477.0012

The need of a more developed financial model, however, could be presented for that target of filmmakers who, having gone through an amateurish initial phase and gotten to a second step, have the need to upgrade the artistic and technical standards of their own productions. The legitimate artistic ambitions do not agree with the absence of a financial model that, therefore, needs the certainty of revenue sources and of a budget proportioned to the real commercial potentialities.

For such reasons, it is easy to understand the necessity, also for the web, of a well-defined financial model. This, rather than being promoted by filmmakers, or by their associations, could find a valuable impulse in the SVoD market, where OTT players are active in releasing original and non-original contents and Online Video Aggregators (OVA) are emerging. OTT and OVA are interested in filling their own platforms of innovative content. In such optic, it is possible to imagine that, in the near future, there could be new players that would put together on specific platforms of web products of audiovisual nature. Such platforms could follow a non-profit model or could individualize models of revenue sharing of advertising proceeds between the platform that takes care of content, the telecom companies and filmmakers. The various mechanisms of sharing between advertising agents, telecom and platforms, together with the weak attention of filmmakers towards the commercial potentiality of their own products and the exploitation of copyrights, do not make it easy to implement financial mechanisms that reward the authorial work of filmmakers. The entry on the market of players able to package baskets of products from different filmmakers would certainly foster the process. In the future, it will be necessary to have more transparency on the types of agreements which platforms stipulate with advertising agents, and of those which the single platforms stipulate with telecom, together with a re-visitation of web products copyrights legal framework.

In the financing process of web products, additionally, an important role could be played by public resources; public support, in fact, should be always more concentrated on cultural and low budget products promoted by young authors. The introduction of fiscal incentives specific for web native audiovisual products, for example, together with direct funds destined to development costs, could represent a valid option for a financial model able to support the growth of the web audiovisual market and young authors.

DOI: 10.1057/9781137378477.0012

Notes

1 The overhead costs represent the share of attributable costs to the two movies; the unsold risk is estimated equal to the cost of production for the single movie ($5).
2 UNESCO (2005); EC (2012).
3 The European Commission has approved a revised version of the Cinema Communication: 2013/C 332/01.
4 Creative Europe is the new EU framework programme for the Cultural and Creative sectors (CCS) for the 2014–2020 Multi-Annual Financial Framework (MFF). Bringing together the previous Culture, MEDIA and MEDIA Mundus programmes under a common framework, it creates a new Guarantee fund to improve access to finance (COM/2011/0786).

DOI: 10.1057/9781137378477.0012

OPEN

8
Financing the Audiovisual Industry

Abstract: *This chapter describes the main financial techniques adopted by financial intermediaries to finance audiovisual productions – such as the slate financing structure and the ticked linked bond – and the use of innovative instruments – such as securitization of rights, crowdfunding and microcredit. These techniques follow the logic of contract discounting rather than gap financing. In this latter case, intermediaries usually prefer to act as lenders, rather than to act as equity investors. The reason is to be found precisely in the logic of risk management. In this perspective, the chapter outlines a taxonomy of financial risks associated with financing the industry and the role of guarantee funds in managing the credit risk exposure.*

La Torre, Mario. *The Economics of the Audiovisual Industry: Financing TV, Film and Web.* Basingstoke: Palgrave Macmillan, 2014. DOI: 10.1057/9781137378477.0013.

8.1 Introduction

The main difference between public and private funding lies in the objectives that motivate investors. Public funding bodies will support the development of the audiovisual market as a component of cultural industry, while private investors will look for profits. This implies a different evaluation of the project or the production company to be financially supported.

It is worth noting that, in general terms, financial intermediaries active in the audiovisual industry follow the logic of *contract discounting*. *Gap financing*, or in other words financing a part of the budget relying on future revenue, is a less common practice, even though in recent years some financiers have developed specific financing techniques to cover the gap. These techniques favour the approach of *project financing*, aimed at funding a single project or a portfolio of projects. The approach of corporate finance, namely, financing a company as a whole, happens very rarely. Intermediaries usually prefer to act as lenders providing funds to cover debts deriving from specified projects, rather than to act as equity investors. The reason is to be found precisely in the logic of risk management. Reduced size of audiovisual companies, low capitalization, short lifespan, often linked to the production of individual projects, are all factors that do not fit corporate finance or equity investments. When possible, however, in the case of more structured companies, corporate financing is applied with the same techniques used for the financing of portfolios of audiovisual projects, but using the company's library as collateral. The choice of equity investment is limited to very few examples.

The purpose of this chapter, therefore, is to outline a preliminary taxonomy of financial risks associated with financing the audiovisual industry and to describe some of the main financial techniques adopted in the credit market and the capital market. It will also be demonstrated why different forms of financing must be based on an analysis of the value of audiovisual products, in particular of their sale price. At this stage, the theory of value and the pricing models outlined in Chapters 5 and 6 become of utmost importance. Without them the finance of the audiovisual industry does not exist.

8.2 Access to finance for the audiovisual industry

Production of audiovisual products is based on high capital-intensity processes that require, in early development stages, high liquidity. In

DOI: 10.1057/9781137378477.0013

financial terms, it means the need to obtain funding in accordance with the budget and in line with the cash flow needed to support the production development.

Financial models of the audiovisual industry actually expose audiovisual firms to a double risk. On one hand, the trend is that soft money is getting harder; constraints on public expenditures have reduced the amount of government subsidies devoted to the audiovisual industry, while the assignment criteria are increasingly oriented towards the assessing of the efficiency of the applying companies. On the other hand, the effect of the financial crisis has shortened the resources deriving from the exploitation of rights, which are strongly dependent on the economic cycle. In these conditions, opening the audiovisual industry to private financing is unavoidable.

The essential requirement for private funding to take place is to verify the sustainability of a project. Investors need to assess the potential return on investment. Revenues determined by the pre-sales mechanism and future revenues estimated on the basis of the possible transfer of the unexploited rights must be considered before determining the rate of return on investment.

In the case of the audiovisual industry, sustainability takes on peculiar features. Firstly, the assessment of future revenues is conditioned by a variable that is difficult to estimate, and that is the success with the audience. It is easy to perceive the difference between estimating the revenues in the case of new products and for sequels or remakes, as well as, for example, estimating future revenues from a film before and after it is released in cinemas; in the latter case, the *box office* can be indicative for estimations of revenues from other exploitation markets.

Secondly, the analysis of the audiovisual industry financial model clearly shows how the above-mentioned considerations should not only refer to the potential revenue sources, but must also take into account commercial and financial relations among the different players of the market. For example, a bank which decides to finance a film project cannot do it without a careful analysis of the distribution deal and the recoupment agreement agreed on between the producer and the distributor. As regards the revenues generated by the film, in fact, the amount the producer will have at its disposal in order to cover the debt depends on the provisions of the distribution deal. The exact understanding of the mechanisms of allocating revenues defined in the distribution agreement becomes for the lending bank the key point of the lending process.

DOI: 10.1057/9781137378477.0013

8.3 Financial risks in financing the audiovisual industry

Financial intermediaries entering the audiovisual industry need to be fully aware of all the risks and of the financial chain of every single project they decide to finance.

Risk management in the audiovisual industry is no different from any risk management in other industrial sectors. The risk is due to the uncertainty regarding future events and their effects in terms of revenues generated by a given project. The risk, therefore, can produce positive or negative effects by increasing or decreasing future revenues. A rational investor will try to measure *ex ante* the level of risk of a given investment, in order to assess whether to invest or not and at what price. Therefore, the risk has two dimensions: the "expected component", that the rational investor expects and incorporates in its decision, and the "unexpected component", that cannot be forecasted. Risk management is responsible for identifying, measuring, managing and controlling risk determinants and all their components.

Financing the audiovisual industry brings with it peculiar risk determinants that make even more complex the risk management process. This is largely due to the nature of "prototype good" of audiovisual products: on the one hand, the production process is difficult to standardize in all is phases, and is often subject to variation due to internal and external circumstances; on the other, the final quality of the product can be largely de-correlated by the quality of the production factors. For these reasons, a taxonomy of the risks associated with financing audiovisual products is needed. In the taxonomy proposed below, each single risk is related to a specific category of traditional financial risks (Figure 8.1).

Audiovisual productions are associated with *business risks*, *operational risks* and *financial risks*. These types of risk impact, directly or indirectly, the ability of the debtor to cover its obligations with revenues and, therefore, affect the return on investment made by the investor who financed the project or company.

Business risks

Firstly, financing audiovisual products exposes the intermediary to a *specific business risk*, a risk that is directly linked to the given project or to the company (*project risk* or *company risk*). Regarding this type of

DOI: 10.1057/9781137378477.0013

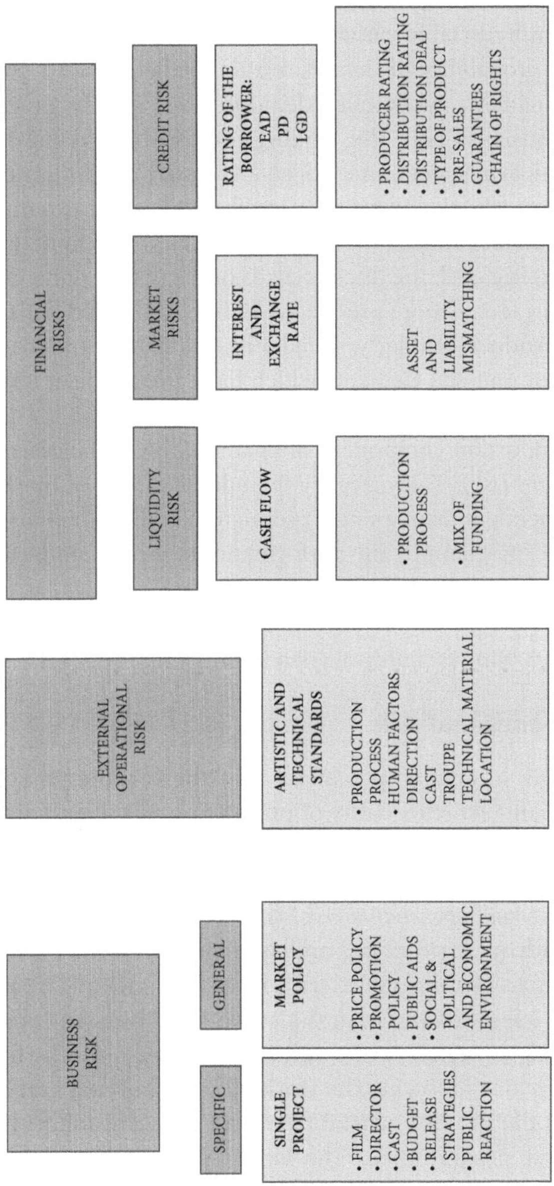

FIGURE 8.1 *Risks and determinants in financing the audiovisual industry*

DOI: 10.1057/9781137378477.0013

risk, it is important to underline how the positive or negative performance of the financed product – or basket of products – is determined by elements that are hard to estimate. The response of the audience remains an unpredictable variable, and such situation makes it difficult to assess the probability of default related to the financed project. The analysis of financing techniques demonstrates how, in order to limit the specific business risk, the lending intermediary requires that the production must respect some covenants based on projections of the available historical data, ensuring a minimum level of revenue predictability. The perfect examples are those projects where famous directors and actors are engaged: the track records of the director and of the main actors allow, in fact, a more precise evaluation of the performance of the audiovisual product. Similarly, sequel projects that reproduce technical, artistic and commercial elements which have already been tested on the public lead to a lower business risk level.

Another important component of business risk is the *general business risk* (or *industry risk*). This category includes a variety of market factors that are independent from a single production and are uncontrollable for the company; for example, the performance of a film can be influenced by market dynamics, including wrong industrial policies (as in the case of too high ticket price), inadequate cultural and education policies, or, indirectly, by economic-political recession.

External operational risk

Every audiovisual company is aware that there is the possibility that the technical and artistic quality of production may result distant from the expected one, or that the production may suffer variations in the schedule or, even worse, that it may not be completed at all. Such risk is part of the *external operational risk*. The occurrence of such events can be due to inadequate processes and systems within the production, as well as to human factors and external or environmental circumstances. The external operational risk in the audiovisual business presents two types of effects: a monetary one and an economic one. The first type is determined by not following the working plan and may imply a financial stress, as the use of financial resources does not follow the timing that had been programmed. The latter type occurs when expenses exceed the budgeted amount, or when the lower quality of the final product results in lower revenues (or, if the project is not completed,

DOI: 10.1057/9781137378477.0013

no revenues at all) and, therefore, no possibility of return for the intermediary.

The transfer of risk to another intermediary is the only possible form of risk management when dealing with external operational risk. Banks active in the audiovisual industry usually manage the operational risk by transferring the risks to specialized intermediaries, such as completion bonders that have the know-how to deal with the completion and delivery risks of the product.

A *completion bond* is a form of contract that guarantees that the product will be completed and delivered as it includes: (a) the agreed production schedule and (b) the levels of the budget established as appropriate. The majority of banks will request a *completion bond* as collateral, but it can also be required by broadcasters, private investors, public bodies or by distributors who have already paid the *minimum guarantee* during the development of the project, or by co-producers. Regardless of the institution that requires the completion bond, the purpose is to hedge against the risk of non-completion of the work resulting in the inability to recover the funds already spent. Among the obligations of the *completion guarantor* are the following:

1) the *completion guarantor* ensures that the producer will complete and deliver the work in accordance with a set of criteria previously approved by the investor regarding the script, schedule and budget;
2) the *completion guarantor* undertakes to ensure financial resources in excess of the approved budget which may become necessary;
3) in case the producer is unable to finish the production, the *completion guarantor* will assume the task of completing it by replacing the producer and the director, if necessary[1], or alternatively, will fully repay to the lender all amounts invested in the production of the work up to that time.

In order to undertake a contractual commitment of this kind, the *completion guarantor* must necessarily examine all the factors affecting the production, such as the story and screenplay, the budget, cash flow, the shooting schedule, the cast and technical crew, locations, insurance policies[2], as well as the financial structure and the individual involvement of each investor. The guarantor may also require an increase in the budget, if it is deemed inconsistent or insufficient. As regards timing, the *completion bond* is signed in conjunction with the request for funding, and certainly before the start of the shooting. In return for the assumed

DOI: 10.1057/9781137378477.0013

risk, the *completion guarantor* is entitled, in addition to receiving a fee, to exercise certain rights, such as being constantly informed on the production and having access to accurate reports related to the budget, cash flow and schedule, as well as the right to exercise a constant monitoring of the locations by engaging, where necessary, technicians and experts on the shooting set. If the monitoring and control reveal constant levels of overspending, the *completion guarantor* has the right to make changes to the cast and crew, and in some extreme cases, the right to substitute the producer and director and to take over their place in the completion of the film. It is in the interest of banks and lenders to make sure that the company providing a *completion bond* has a good reputation and a brilliant track record. But above all, it is important to verify whether the guarantor's financial solidity is enough to fulfil its commitments. To this end, the *completion guarantor* often transfers part of the risks taken against the bank and the producer to an insurance company by entering into a re-insurance called "*cut-through*" that gives the bank the right to take action against the insurer in the event that the *completion guarantor* is unable to meet its contractual obligations. The cost attributable to the *completion bond* varies depending strongly on the intrinsic characteristics of each production, the track record of the producer making the request and the general conditions on the *completion bond* market at the time of signing[3]. Should it be necessary for the *completion guarantor* to anticipate some money in order to complete the film, it will have the priority, over all other investors excluding the bank, to recover the sum from revenues generated by the film.

Financial risks

Financial risks in the audiovisual financing are attributable to the typical liquidity, market and credit risks.

Liquidity risk is due to the possibility that the inflows may not be able to cover the outflows. Film productions are characterized by strong financial stress which is concentrated, in particular, in the early stages of production and are determined by a mismatching between inflows and outflows. The gap between the timing and the amounts of incoming and outgoing cash flows is a natural condition of audiovisual productions and may affect the debtor's ability to pay its debt.

Therefore, the loan should be aimed at favouring the debtor's monetary equilibrium, allowing it to avoid financial stress likely to affect

DOI: 10.1057/9781137378477.0013

its solvency. In this regard, three conditions are relevant: the timing of financing, forms of use and the amortization schedule. It is crucial that the debtor is able to use the granted funds according to the financial needs dictated by the production cycle. Financial crisis of the debtor, in fact, could adversely affect its ability to repay the loan.

Market risks are determined by changes in interest rates and exchange rates affecting the income or the value of the assets of an audiovisual company or of a single project. Changing interest or exchange rates may have a possible impact on the overall capacity of the borrower to pay its debt. The company's exposure to market risks, including in relation to individual projects, will be the subject of risk management policies implemented by the company itself; the efficacy of risk management policies will affect the credit rating expressed by a bank or any other potential lender. The risk of interest rates is relevant when the production or audiovisual company is heavily indebted. In such a case, a change in interest rates can have a negative impact on the ability to repay the financial obligations.

The exchange rate risk assumes significance in the case of international productions within which the budget is expressed in a foreign currency.

Market risks are a critical variable of audiovisual productions as, in most cases, production companies do not have the internal expertise to manage them. The techniques of asset and liability management at the base of the management of market risks, in fact, require a specific know-how and an *ad hoc* organizational structure. In practice, therefore, production companies resort to external companies – in some cases, the lending banks themselves – to assist the companies in managing risks with advice and financial products suitable for their specific needs.

The *credit risk* contextualized in the audiovisual industry leads to its most significant manifestation, that is, insolvency. The *insolvency loss effect* is, in fact, the most common outcome of credit risk.[4]

The credit risk assessment finds a crucial variable in evaluating the borrower's rating. The evaluation of the *counterpart credit risk* refers to the typical determinants of credit risk and in particular to the probability of default (PD) of the borrower and to the loss given default (LGD).[5] The estimation of the PD implies an initial difficulty in the exact identification of the counterpart that shall be evaluated. This is particularly true for the film industry. The analysis of the distribution deal has clarified how the agreements between producer and distributor influence the sharing of the revenue flows between production and distribution. The producer's

DOI: 10.1057/9781137378477.0013

chances of receiving its shares, as well as the level of coverage of production costs, shall not only depend on the market performance of the film, but also on the recoupment agreements stated in the distribution deal and on the exploiting skills of the distributor on those markets that follow the theatrical one. This shall be confirmed in the case that the distribution deal slows down the recovery of the producer's shares, as it happens in the *net deal* contract. Therefore, for a lender that needs to estimate the rate of return of his investment, it is essential to globally evaluate the counterparts that are involved in the project and the agreements with such counterparts. Another difficulty in measuring counterpart credit risk is represented by the typology of guarantees that are required by the intermediary in order to reduce the LGD. On a market such as the audiovisual industry, where borrowers and lenders generally don't know each other, real assets guarantees are normally required. However, audiovisual firms – including companies that work on an established basis and not on specifically designed structures for single projects – do not generally invest much in property. Hence, collaterals made of real assets are distant from the nature of the production cycle of this industry and, consequently, are hardly applied. Nevertheless, typical assets of the audiovisual companies are represented by the exploitation rights to their library of products. These rights represent – together with pre-sales contracts – the most natural form of guarantee. The identification of the rights of the borrower, and their evaluation, require, however, time and the know-how that could not be compatible with the urgent financial needs of the borrower and with the expertise of lenders. Consequently, the availability in the credit market of institutions and professionals able to carry out – at affordable costs and in reasonable time – an evaluation of the library is of paramount importance. The unavailability of such players would limit the credit guarantee to the agreed pre-sales contracts, while the full use of the rights concerning the company's library would be possible only for few financial transactions.

For the financial intermediaries, the exposure to credit risk is of utmost importance in the credit policies. Supervisory authorities, in fact, require intermediaries to set aside regulatory capital in relation to the risk levels of loans granted.[6] The higher the risk, the more capital must be set aside. According to the rules of prudential regulation, financing audiovisual companies is placed within the higher levels of risk, both because of the lack of capitalization of the companies and because of the intangible nature of the exploitation rights that are not considered high-quality guarantees. This fact translates into a higher cost for

DOI: 10.1057/9781137378477.0013

intermediaries – measurable in terms of regulatory capital absorbed by the single credit exposure.

For intermediaries active in the audiovisual industry, the best policy to manage credit risks is to adopt a portfolio approach allowing for diversification strategies. A "pool of projects approach" – applied to different projects of the same company or to single projects that are promoted by various companies provides, through diversification, a lower exposure not only to credit risk and financial risks in general, but also to business risk and operational risk.

Finally, considering the general business risk, the intermediary has to avoid the concentration risk; this would derive from building up a loan portfolio with a high percentage of loans granted to the audiovisual industry. In this perspective, it is useful to carry out an adequate evaluation of the audiovisual business share on total loans.

In addition to management policies, in practice, intermediaries resort to specific financial schemes limiting their risk exposure. Many of the financial structures, for example, include the use of a special purpose vehicle (SPV). Its purpose is to isolate the financed project from the producer's budget, limiting the intermediary's exposure to the counterparty credit risk. In this way, the PD is attributable to a single project only and the LGD is not influenced by the production and distribution companies. Similar structures are particularly useful in financing co-productions for which estimates of the creditworthiness of various productions involved can be particularly difficult and laborious.

8.4 How to finance the audiovisual industry: products and markets

Intermediaries financing film productions can intervene in two different ways: *contract discounting and gap financing*, differing in the degree of involvement on the part of the intermediary, in terms of both risks and expected return, as well as in terms of requested requirements and collaterals[7].

Contract discounting

Following the discount approach, banks and financial intermediaries discount the future revenues deriving from pre-sale contracts already

DOI: 10.1057/9781137378477.0013

signed and that the producer has entered into with other parties before addressing the intermediary. In this case, banks do not provide additional financial resources for the production but merely act as a liquidity provider. In other words, banks make available financial resources that would only be liquidated at a later time. The ability to get a discount to existing agreements, which provide for payments but only in conjunction with the completion of the audiovisual product and its subsequent release on exploitation markets, enables the producer to find resources that can be used to cover the costs related to the production phase, generally associated to a certain degree of financial stress. Existing agreements are usually valuated below their paper value. From the banks' point of view, if properly implemented, discount contracts are considered not too risky, and at the same time, rewarding transactions. Usually, the discount rate is determined on the basis of a benchmark market rate[8] and by adding a commonly agreed spread that may vary depending on the levels of risk taken, the quality of the guarantees provided and the track record of the producer. In addition, banks will charge the producer with a lump sum commission (fee), organizational and managerial costs incurred and the costs of legal expenses required for the discount.

Gap financing

In this second scenario, intermediaries are exposed to a greater degree of credit risk, as they undertake to provide the missing financial resources for the project counting on future revenues deriving from future contracts. Intermediaries, in this case, lend the amounts primarily based on sales estimates of the exploitation rights to the product on different territories. The term "gap" refers to the fact that banks and intermediaries provide financial coverage for any difference (shortfall) between the funding already found and the amount necessary for the production, thereby providing the missing funds for the final coverage of the budget, providing the so-called "missing financing". The gap is calculated as[9]:

$$\text{GAP} = [\text{Total Budget Requirements} - \text{Already Received Financing}] \quad 8.1$$

In these cases, banks will accept higher levels of risk, taking into account also the estimates made by independent sales agents on the value of product rights on those territories and exploitation markets where the product has not been sold yet. In general terms, based on the elements such as cast, director, genre, production and budget, sales agents prepare

DOI: 10.1057/9781137378477.0013

estimates for the different territories. Banks will grant the necessary funding only if convinced by the feasibility of these estimates, favouring the agents of well-established reputation in the industry that will commit themselves to sell the product in the countries considered in their predictions. In such a context, the possibility of using gap financing works well for those titles which have clear potential sales and business opportunities on a wide range of markets, also internationally. Usually, intermediaries will require that the values indicating the revenues from the sale of film rights in multiple territories, and on different markets in the same region, indicate the existence of significant margins that would provide for the repayment of the loan[10].

Also in gap financing banks and financial intermediaries require the priority on the waterfall of revenues from the product funded. But, intermediaries may also accept a "parallel" recovery to other lenders, such as in the case of a product funded by the State or other public institutions. We should keep in mind that it is a rather costly and challenging form of financing, given the high costs the intermediaries apply in the form of commissions (fees), reimbursement of expenses and, more importantly, in terms of interest rates negotiated for the loan granted that are higher than those applied in the contract discounting and established on a case-by-case basis. In the Anglo-Saxon financial context, the intermediaries may require the presence of an additional independent party, a sort of *super partes* risk manager which, given a contractually established commission[11], will express a judgment on the adequacy of sales estimates made by the sales agents and will certify the quality and commercial viability of the project, exerting also a function of monitoring and control over the making of the product, as well as on subsequent modes of economic exploitation from which the revenues to cover the loan come.

In practice, the banks and financial intermediaries financing audiovisual productions often use a combination of the two approaches described. They provide liquidity through the discount of existing contracts and possibly integrate it with the provision of gap financing for an amount that should not exceed 20–30% of the budget, thus giving rise to structures of "hybrid" debt financing.

Bank lending structures

While in the United States and in the UK financial intermediaries have been actively supporting the audiovisual business for quite a long time, in continental Europe relationships between banks, financial

DOI: 10.1057/9781137378477.0013

intermediaries, institutional investors and film industry have been seriously taken into consideration only recently. Financial innovation has produced new products used to fill the financial gap of a project.

Some typical financial structures adopted by international banks to finance films and television products – mainly fiction – will be described below. These structures are adaptable, with proper precautions, also for the purposes of other television products and those web products that generate enough revenues to cover the cost of the loan.

In order to deal with the most incisive peculiarities of audiovisual productions, namely, the unpredictable future incomes, financial intermediaries have designed some financial tools and techniques that help achieve two objectives:

- to separate the financed assets from the debtor's balance sheet, thus segregating the individual assets and rights on which to rely for the repayment of the financing provided;
- to break down and redistribute risks according to risk sharing models that allow to assign the risks to the most appropriate types of investors.

Segregation of assets on one hand and risk diversification on the other seem to be the drivers of the debt financing products primarily used by banks.

In particular, in this paragraph, the following financial products will be taken into consideration:

- single film project financing,
- revenues discounting credit facility and portfolio project financing, and
- leasing and microcredit.

Single film financing

Single film financing (Figure 8.2) consists in financing the production of a single project and can be issued in a pre-production phase, as well as during production.[12]

The amount of the loan is defined according to the value of the rights that are sold in advance and, in the case of a film project, is independent from *box office* results. If compared to a traditional credit line, single project financing includes some important differences. The structure uses a special purpose vehicle (SPV) which has two functions: (a) it acquires from the producer the ownership of the cash

DOI: 10.1057/9781137378477.0013

flow generated by the negotiated rights on which the amount of the financing depends; (b) it provides the servicing of the financial flow of the transaction. Actually, first the bank acquires the cash flow rights, then provides a loan for the SPV, which uses it to pay the producer for the transfer. Subsequently, the SPV receives from distributors the cash flow deriving from the acquired rights and transfers them to the bank in order to pay back the loan.

This structure allows the financing institution to identify financial risks according to two main variables: (a) the counterpart credit risk regarding the distributors involved in the transaction – since the financial flow that is earmarked to pay back the loan depends on the ability of the distributor to exploit the rights and to comply with the transfer of money to the SPV; (b) the risk of non-completion of the work: the essential condition for the distributor to fulfil its commitments set out in the distribution deal – leading to the ability of the financial intermediary to be refunded is the actual completion of the film – is the creation of a master copy allowing for the economic exploitation of the product.

This type of structure allows controlling and limiting some of the typical risks of film financing. First of all, the transfer to SPV of the contractual rights allows separating the specific project from the producer's

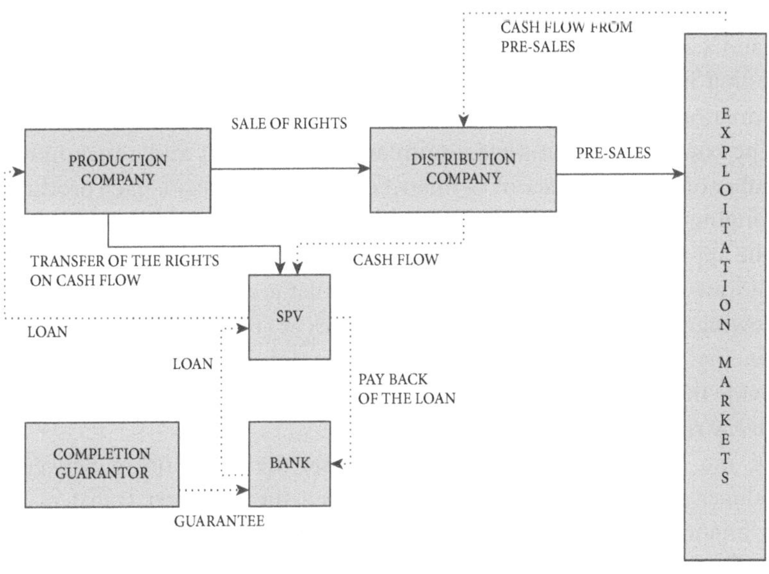

FIGURE 8.2 *Single film financing*

DOI: 10.1057/9781137378477.0013

balance sheet, so that the financing institution can focus its activity on a single project, rather than on the credit rating of the company. Moreover, segregation of the assets that represent the collateral of the transaction provides a more transparent cash flow and facilitates risk sharing with third counterparts. Usually, such structure provides, in collaboration with a bank, the presence of an intermediary – normally an insurance company – that offers a completion guarantee for the risks related to the completion of the project. By doing so, the financing bank can be sure that any technical or artistic problems occurring during the production shall not prejudice the payback of the loan. The completion guarantor, upon the payment of a predetermined fee, agrees to finish the film in case budgets and deadlines are not met during the original production.

A systemic approach – which is quite common among the most dynamic intermediaries operating in the industry – suggests the use of portfolio project financing, oriented towards the support of a large number of projects proposed by the same company, as well as of projects of different companies.

Revenue discounting credit facility and film slate financing

In the case of portfolio approach, many financial techniques can be used; however, for taxonomic simplicity, it is possible to identify two options: the *revenue discounting credit facility* and the *film slate financing* (Figures 8.3 and 8.4)[13]. Both structures provide a company with a revolving credit line that is guaranteed by the rights of a basket of movies during pre-production and production.

The contract sets out a maximum available amount and a maximum number of products that can be financed in a certain period. Each product belonging to the initial pool – as well as to the revolving one – is subject to the approval of the financing institution. The borrowing company can withdraw in order to finance the projects that are included in the pool, following payback schedules and procedures as stated. As for single film financing, also in this case a completion guarantor is present in order to provide the lending intermediary with insurance on the completion and delivery risks of the projects.

In the revenue discount facility scheme, the relationship between producer and financing institution is direct: the producer transfers to the financial intermediary the rights concerning the pre-sales-based cash flow. In slate film financing the same function found in single film financing is carried out by a SPV. Therefore, only in the first case banks have the possibility to take a direct legal action against the producer.

DOI: 10.1057/9781137378477.0013

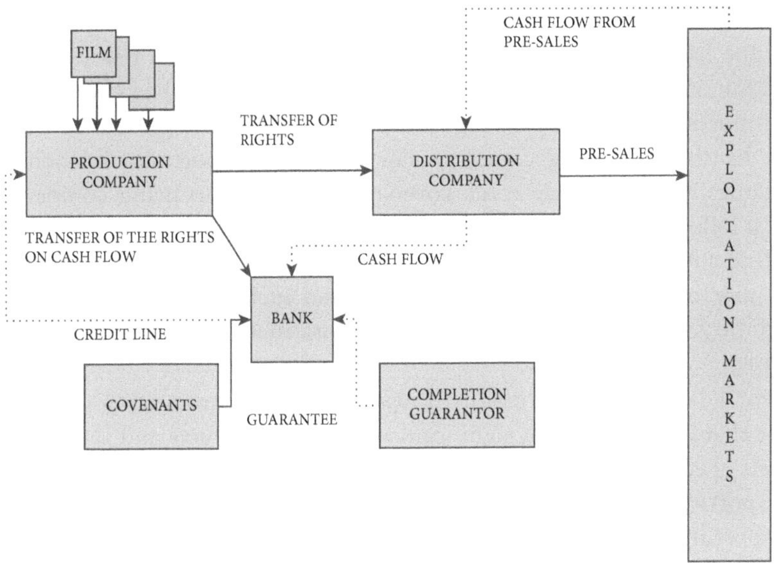

FIGURE 8.3 *Revenue discount facility*

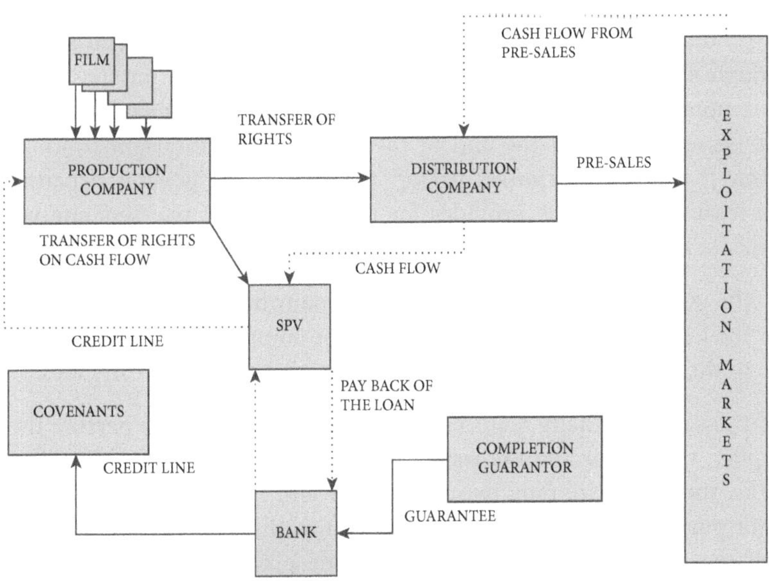

FIGURE 8.4 *Film slate financing*

DOI: 10.1057/9781137378477.0013

Destining funds to a portfolio of films, rather than to single projects, on one hand allows the financing institution to perform a risk diversification among different typologies of products, but on the other hand, it imposes a higher monitoring level of the project management carried out by the borrowing company. For this reason, portfolio financing schemes always include some covenants that the borrowing company must follow. Among the most common covenants required, it is possible to find a minimum level of equity invested by the producer, a minimum number of printed copies for each product included in the portfolio and the adequacy of the distribution network that is used for selling the rights.

Portfolio financing is mainly designed for those production companies that can guarantee a significant number of products and satisfying levels of equity. However, besides its application on a well-defined target, the portfolio approach can be considered as a valuable model also for supporting smaller companies or single projects. Careful consideration of the managerial attitude of the borrower and the application of a set of covenants should represent the essential elements of any audiovisual project financing.

Leasing

In particular cases, banks have used a leasing agreement to finance the production of audiovisual works, mostly films.[14] In general terms, through a lease agreement one party (Lessor) agrees to purchase and contemporarily to lease an asset acquired from a supplier to a third party (the Lessee), which at the end of the contract, has the right (option) to buy it at a predetermined price.[15] Technically, the general structure of a leasing transaction provides for the existence of two separate yet connected contracts:

1) the purchase by which the leasing company buys a certain asset;
2) the Lease itself, through which the same company leases the asset to the user (lessee) against the payment of monthly or yearly fees.

The transaction usually requires a structure involving three parties: the supplier, the Lessor and the lessee. However, in the case of audiovisual works, the actors are only two (the owner and Lessor), since the good is not purchased by a third party, but is directly produced by the user itself that, in this case, coincides with the producer (direct lease or sale and leaseback, Figure 8.5). In this way, the producer immediately

DOI: 10.1057/9781137378477.0013

obtains the cash needed from the proceeds of the sale and, at the same time, preserves the rights to the asset (the work produced) thanks to the leasing relationship allowing the producer to repurchase the asset by paying the fees and by exercising the option upon the termination of the contract. The contract stipulates that at the agreed time, the user/producer can regain ownership of the asset sold by the intermediary (the movie), pursuant to a purchase option included in the contract. Lease transactions on an audiovisual product essentially involve:

- a production company that transfers the ownership of an audiovisual product in exchange for an immediate cash benefit and is required to make escalating periodical rental payments to the Lessor; the producer benefits by receiving the purchase price, whilst being able to, at the same time, exploit the film commercially;
- a Lessor that is a specialized financial intermediary, purchaser of master negatives/tapes of a completed audiovisual work that, immediately after buying the work from the producer, leases it back to the same producer and receives a fee;
- in some cases, a bank or a specialized intermediary engaged by the leasing company for the medium-/long-term financing. In most cases, the rental payments must be secured by way of a bank guarantee or a standby letter of credit.

Usually, in an international context, and in more financially developed cases, the transfer takes place through a special purpose vehicle (SPV) that acquires ownership rights from the producer on behalf of the intermediary and, at the same time, pays the monetary value to the producer, which in turn agrees to pay a fee periodically to the lessor. It is normally the producer who chooses the moment to sign a leasing contract, in relation to a given product, the contractual duration of the transaction (which on average varies from 36 to 48, up to a maximum of 60 months) and the frequency of payments.[16] However, a prerequisite for such a contract to be signed is that the work is finished, or at least a large part of the footage is in postproduction. The main advantage for the producer is the liberation of financial resources, the payment of which is not strongly correlated and dependent on the *box office* results, and if exploited consistently, enables the company to start new investments and to finance new projects. It is due to the fact that the economic benefit arising from the immediate financial resources that the leasing transaction frees for the producer does not manifest itself

DOI: 10.1057/9781137378477.0013

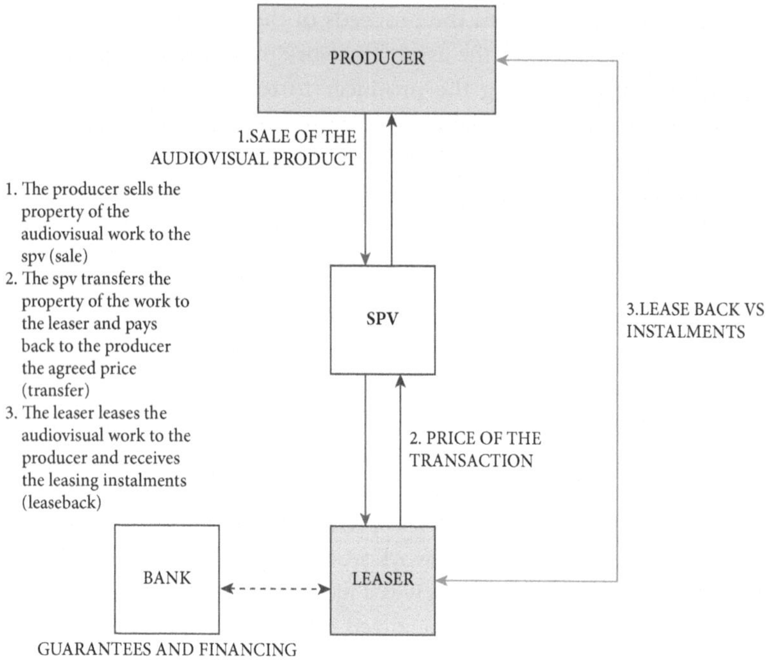

FIGURE 8.5 *Leasing of audiovisual products*

on the financial structure of the film involved in the lease (which must already be completed in order to access the transaction[17]), but presumably the liquidity that is made available from the transaction will benefit the funding of future projects in progress, or in other words, the resources freed up by the leasing contract will form the financial structure of other films. And therefore, this method of financing is only useful for companies that regularly devote themselves to film productions and portfolios investing in a long-term perspective, and not the firms established with the aim of producing a single movie and whose existence is conditioned upon completion of a single project. On the other hand, intermediaries specializing in lease agreements will evaluate the costs, fees and fairness of the transaction not only based on the characteristics of the film being object of the lease term, or its expected *box office* returns, but also on a function of the economic and financial solidity of the production company and the value of the library in its possession. In other words, the overall risk of a lease, from the point of view of the lessor, is evaluated by weighting the risk relative to the production company with the one related to the product.

DOI: 10.1057/9781137378477.0013

Microcredit

In general terms, microcredit is a small loan granted to individuals – or a group of individuals – excluded from the traditional financial system, to finance a micro-entrepreneurial activity.[18] Traditional guarantees are absent and often substituted by guarantee funds, usually provided by States. The traditional microcredit market derives from the microcredit initiatives carried out in developing countries to help the so called "poorest of the poor". In such a context of financial exclusion, microcredit represents a valid tool of inclusive credit policies, because it is capable of overcoming the traditional logic of customer selection utilized by banks and financial intermediaries. The lending methodology in microcredit widely differs from that of traditional finance, and the creditworthiness analysis of the borrowers focuses mainly on qualitative factors.

With this in mind, microcredit may result a useful financial instrument for all those young authors and independent small audiovisual firms that are not able to access the traditional banking market and to provide traditional guarantees.

In the audiovisual industry, the traditional microcredit structure can be adapted to meet the needs of small productions. Microcredit programmes can be financed both by governmental bodies and private investors. Funds can be channelled through microfinance institutions – where the legislation provides for this type of intermediary – or traditional banks, while capacity building institutions may carry out the qualitative analysis of the borrowers, also providing technical assistance to borrowers during the whole process.

Several industrial countries have implemented specific microcredit regulations in order to foster the microcredit market: in Europe this is the case, among others, for France, Italy and Romania. In these countries, microcredit may result as a valid alternative to traditional credit, especially to finance web audiovisual products, or even the start-up of young production and distribution companies. It is worth noting, anyway, that microcredit is a credit product suitable only for those firms or projects that are able to generate enough revenues to repay the financial costs of the debt.

The development of a microcredit market for the audiovisual industry is largely dependent on the promotion of guarantee funds and the implementation of specific legislation which would allow for microfinance institutions to enter the market.

DOI: 10.1057/9781137378477.0013

Access to capital market

In countries with "well-established" financial systems, the capital market, even for companies active in the audiovisual sector, is one of the most important financing channels, and placement of debt securities and shares to the public is the most common way to recover capital.

The importance of the stock market for audiovisual firms seems to be finally established in the United States and in most Anglo-Saxon countries, where several companies are listed on the Stock Exchange and raise capital on the equity market.

The access to capital markets is still at a very early stage in continental Europe, where very few firms are listed on the Stock Exchange and only few companies regularly issue debt securities. Among the reasons that most are frequently discouraged from entering the Stock Exchange are the costs and the fear of a new governance model. Shareholders who control the company fear having to suffer the possible interference from third parties. For audiovisual firms, still experiencing a bank-oriented market, the direct access to the stock market seems to be premature while it could be a useful alternative strategy in the future.

Nevertheless, in recent years, a number of new financial instruments have been developed by financial intermediaries to help audiovisual firms to attract funds on capital markets from institutional investors and from private and retail investors. The use of these new financial techniques have been stimulated by the securitization process experienced by financial markets, which provides, for the financial needs of the borrower, the issue and placement of negotiable securities. In such perspective, financial instruments for the audiovisual industry can be divided in two typologies: *theatrical performance instruments*, which guarantee a return rate that depends on the theatrical revenue, and *full rights performance instruments*, where the revenue depends on a wider exploitation of the film rights. As a consequence, the first type of financing is restricted to film financing.

The list of most commonly used financial products to raise funds on capital markets for audiovisual productions includes: ticket linked bonds, asset-backed securitization (ABS), investment funds and crowdfunding.

Ticket-linked bonds

The first category, the instrument that has been experimented also on the markets of continental Europe, is the so called *ticket-linked bond*

DOI: 10.1057/9781137378477.0013

(Figure 8.6). This short-term film bond is issued in order to support film production, and it has a yield that depends on the *box office* revenue of the film obtained in a defined market, and for a determined period, which corresponds to the maturity of the bond.[19] In its basic structure, the ticket-linked bond is issued as a zero coupon bond. The potential yield on maturity of the bond consists in the capital and in the interest paid to investors; both capital and interest are calculated as percentage of the number of sold tickets. In fact, for each ticket sold, a defined percentage of the revenue is transferred to the investors of the bond. The amount that the investor will receive on maturity will be equal to:

$$CS = n° \; Bv \; (\%Pb) \qquad 8.1$$

where:

CS = capital and interest on maturity

n° Bv = Number of sold tickets

%Pb = percentage of the price of the ticket transferred to the investors.

Film bonds – generally placed among institutional investors – can be issued at the early stage of the film production, as well as during the advanced production phase. The maturity of the bond depends on the time of issue and on the corresponding production phase of the film and shall be as long as the distance in time between the issue of the bond and the movie's *premiere*. The amount of the issue depends on the film budget and on the resulting financial gap to be covered. The ticket-linked bond can be used to finance a single project or a portfolio of projects. It can be issued to support the production or the distribution. Since the revenue is linked to the theatrical collection, this instrument adapts particularly to the financing of projects that can guarantee a minimum level of predictability of the theatrical return. Therefore, the ticket-linked bond finds its best application in supporting films with important cast and director or sequel projects.

For the arranger, the ticket-linked bond represents an instrument which facilitates the diversification of the risk, since it is transferred and redistributed between the investors of the bond; at same time, the arranger diversifies its revenues which, in the case of this specific transaction, consist of commissions related to the packaging of the programme.

For investors, the bond represents an alternative investment with an average maturity of about 18 months and with no correlation with traditional investments.

DOI: 10.1057/9781137378477.0013

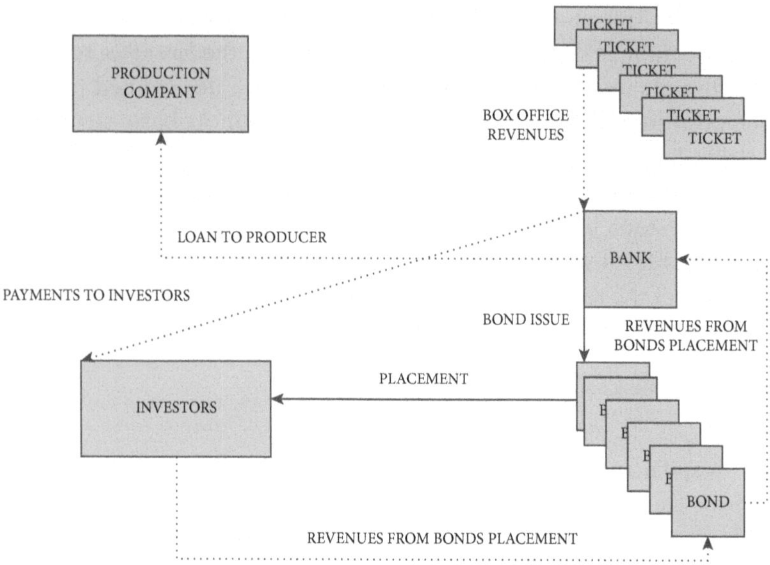

FIGURE 8.6 *Ticket-linked bonds*

For film companies, the ticket-linked bond represents a valid alternative financial instrument for those projects that have good revenue predictability.

Asset-backed securitization

The *asset-backed securitization* (ABS) represents one of the most sophisticated forms of financing available for the audiovisual sector. The ABS is a technique that allows a company (originator) to transfer a pool of assets to a Special Purpose Vehicle (SPV), which finances the transfer by issuing and placing negotiable financial instruments on the capital market.[20] For companies operating in the audiovisual business, the assets involve audiovisual rights stored in their balance sheets, or that shall derive from future productions. For such reason, ABS is a financial technique that can be used by production companies, as well as by distribution firms.

In its most traditional structure, audiovisual rights securitization considers as the originator a production company that transfers a portfolio of rights to an SPV (Figure 8.7). The SPV then issues an amount of asset-backed securities (ABSs) which equals the price of the rights' transfer and places such securities on the market, generally to institutional

DOI: 10.1057/9781137378477.0013

investors. Throughout the duration of the transaction, the revenues that are generated by the exploitation of rights are used to pay the investors.

ABS represents a useful financial technique for those companies – or consortiums of companies – operating in the audiovisual industry, which have a library value that is high enough to justify the costs of implementing an ABS programme. For the production and distribution companies, asset securitization allows cash conversion of the balance sheet assets, and it generates liquidity that can be used for the financing of the production cycle, as well as for the reduction of the financial debt. Such liquidity has a funding cost which may result lower than the borrowing rate of the originator. Asset segregation, in fact, ensures a funding cost that is proportional to the quality of the assets and to the guarantees included in the specific ABS structure, and does not take into account the standing of the originator.

It is useful to point out that, in order to carry out a successful ABS programme, it is necessary to follow certain rules that cannot be disregarded. First of all, every ABS projected for the audiovisual market

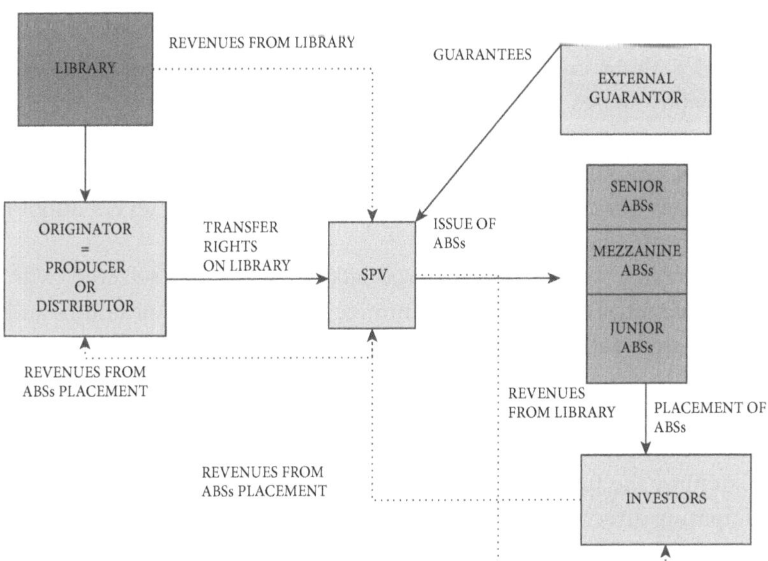

FIGURE 8.7 *Securitization of audiovisual rights*

DOI: 10.1057/9781137378477.0013

must guarantee the certainty of the chain of rights – which means that its object must consist in a package of rights on which the ownership is undoubtedly held by the originator. Secondly, a balanced and truthful evaluation must be carried out on the portfolio of rights.

Finally, it is necessary that the structure of the transaction can guarantee certainty on how the exploitation of the underlying rights will be performed in order to guarantee the expected performance and the regularity of the payback flows of the securitization.

Investment funds

Investment funds represent a way of raising financial resources that allow audiovisual companies to finance their needs; at the same time, individuals and institutional investors may invest their savings into a basket of projects, taking advantage of any existing tax benefits.

Investors are willing to channel their resources towards a dual objective:

a) the search for a profitable investment that would not be correlated to the performance of other traditional industries;
b) the opportunity to take advantage of tax benefits, usually associated with the investment.

The fund is divided into shares, pertaining to a plurality of investors and managed without customized treatment, by a management company. Investors buy shares of the fund, and their money is used to cover the budget of a pool of audiovisual products. It should be clarified that investment funds also adopt an approach of gap financing, under which funding does not cover the entire production budget but serves only to cover a certain percentage of it.

The fund invests in a pool of products, appropriately selected, with various characteristics, so as to minimize the probability of failure and maximize high returns. Once these products are completed, marketed and begin to generate revenue, investors recover the amount initially paid plus a return that can be equal to a percentage of the proceeds, or can be calculated as percentage of the paid-up capital, depending on the extent of the funding and the structure of the fund. In addition to participating directly in the revenue generated by the products financed, usually the Fund has also a share in the ownership of the products.

Each fund must also define an exit strategy as having a duration it needs to emerge definitively from their investments before deadline.

DOI: 10.1057/9781137378477.0013

This requires being able to resell one's shares of the property to producers, or to third-party investors, rather than resorting to a securitization of rights.

For an investor, the attractiveness of a fund lies in the seriousness and competence with which the pool of projects to be funded are analysed and which should be chosen so as to allow a minimization of the risk of commercial failure and burdens. Naturally, tax benefits, usually associated with this kind of funds, represent a protective cushion from any losses or leverage of future revenues.

To summarize, the potential of any investment fund may be reduced to five variables:

- *track record* of the management of the fund, and the production companies who routinely work with the fund;
- *instruments and hedging policies*, which can generally take the form of completion bonds, insurance on the cast and director, pre-sales, estimates of an independent sales agent, careful preparation of the waterfall of repayments and hedging against currency risk;
- *artistic quality and commercial potential* of the products financed;
- the *degree of diversification* of the product portfolio;
- the presence of *tax benefits* associated with the investment.

In the audiovisual industry, there are different examples of private equity firms that have taken the form of a closed-ended investment fund, whose shares are subscribed at an early stage of the fundraising. Once the amount of resources set as an objective of the fund is reached, the management company closes the collection and the investment begins.

In the light of the changes that have taken place in public policies supporting the audiovisual industry, the possibility of creating a fund of mixed private and public capital seems an interesting opportunity. In such a scheme, the public body, or the State directly, may subscribe junior shares and work as "lender of last resort" for private investors; moreover, it would have the advantage of participating in an initiative with the perspective of profit, with possible economic return; besides, this kind of investment could generate a leverage effect greater than that derived from traditional public grants.

Finally, if well planned, investment funds for the audiovisual industry are also appealing to a vast range of retail investors, as they can attract not only those motivated by purely economic purposes, but also individuals driven

DOI: 10.1057/9781137378477.0013

by a strong passion for the audiovisual market, as they believe it to be socially relevant to invest in an industry that produces "cultural" products.

Crowdfunding platforms

Crowdfunding – as the combination of words *crowd* and *funding* suggests – is a process of financing from the bottom. The innovative element of *crowdfunding* is the means by which it is made: the *web*. In essence, the *web* becomes the place where every person in need of money to finance their business idea, or to fulfil personal needs, can appeal to investors and lenders around the world willing to trust them. The meeting between borrowers and lenders is possible through web platforms. *Crowdfunding* is based on a belief that on financial markets there are resources available which are not channelled through traditional financial intermediaries.

Crowdfunding platforms can work in different ways (Figure 8.8).

Accordingly to their objectives, it is possible to identify four types of *crowdfunding*:[21]

1. *donation model*: is generally adopted by non-profit organizations to fund projects from which contributors do not seek revenues;
2. *reward-based model*: requires that investors receive a reward in the form of benefits or gadgets;
3. *social lending model*: investors receive back capital plus interests. Investors and beneficiaries are regarded, to all intents and purposes, as lender and borrower;
4. *equity-based model*: the investor does neither a donation nor a loan, but buys shares of a company: a real investment in venture capital.

As regards the audiovisual industry, the most feasible models of *crowdfunding* are mainly the donation and the reward-based model. These two types, in fact, are able to attract those investors who are inspired by the desire to feel part of the production process of an audiovisual work and do not require additional return. In order to realize the emotional aspiration, these investors are satisfied even if they do not receive any remuneration, or if they simply get gadgets and benefits related to the product. Different experiences of audiovisual crowdfunding have already been tested on different markets and are characterized by a spirit of non-profit donors. Given the nature of this financial support, *crowdfunding* falls into a category of audiovisual financing tools for *art house* products that are promoted by independent producers, often at the first experience. And therefore, it is used for products such as short films and web-native products. There are, however, rare but

DOI: 10.1057/9781137378477.0013

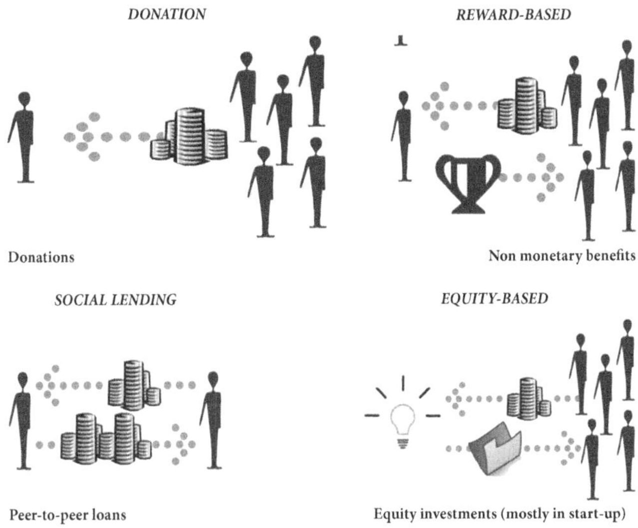

FIGURE 8.8 *Crowdfunding models*

high-profile examples of established authors resorting to *crowdfunding* that have also enjoyed significant success.

Crowdfunding, in the form of social lending and equity, can be seen as one complementary source of funding for medium-high budget products and as a significant funding strategy for *art house* and web audiovisual products. In the future, the recourse to web platforms could be used also by banks and financial intermediaries in combination with more traditional financial structures of bank lending, microcredit, as well as investment funds, especially for those projects with significant potential of future revenues.

The role of guarantee funds and fiscal incentives

Guarantee funds are a necessary tool for the provision of credit to businesses that have a low credit rating, and that do not have real or personal collaterals, as for audiovisual firms. According to this, for audiovisual firms, guarantee funds can be considered a *conditio sine qua non* for access to finance.

For a guarantee fund to work, some essential parameters need to be established. In particular: the *coverage ratio*, the *leverage* rate and the *percentage of provision* to the fund.

The *coverage ratio* of a loan is the loan ratio covered by the guarantee; it never reaches 100% of the nominal value of the loan itself, and represents

DOI: 10.1057/9781137378477.0013

a policy choice of the promoters of the fund. This choice has an impact on the maximum number of payable guarantees. The higher the percentage of coverage, the lower the number of loans guaranteed. The *leverage ratio* of a fund represents its multiplier effect – or how much of the total volume of loans guaranteed may exceed the nominal amount of the fund. This leverage is justified by the fact that it assumes a default rate of less than 100%. The higher the leverage ratio, the wider the maximum expansion of the fund – that is the number and volume of loans warrantable by the fund. Finally, the sustainability of the fund requires that it be fed as the guarantees are being paid. A portion of the guarantee provided must be set aside to ensure the availability of resources in the event of borrower's default.

The example below assumes a guarantee fund with resources amounting to €100 (Table 8.1).

Suppose that the maximum amount of a single loan is fixed at €10, and that the coverage ratio is 80%, while the leverage ratio is equal to 3, and the percentage of provision to the fund is fixed at 20% of the guarantee (option 1). The fund would finance guarantees for €8 on each loan (10 x 0.8). Given the amount of the fund, it can be deduced that the maximum number of loans warrantable would be equal to 37.5 [(100 x 3)/(10 x 0.8)] for a maximum amount of loans secured by €375 (10 x 37.5) and an accounting provision equal to 60 [(10 x 0.8 x 37.5) x 0.2]. If the leverage was lower or equal to 2 (option 2), the number and volume of guaranteed loans would be lower, and would be equal to 25 and 250, and the provision would equal to 40.

If, in contrast, the coverage ratio was lower, suppose equal to 50% (option 3), the fund would finance guarantees of €5 for each loan. In this case, the number and maximum volume of loans warrantable would increase significantly and would be equal to 60 and 600, while the provision would always be equal to 60.

TABLE 8.1 *The functioning of a guarantee fund*

ASSUMPTIONS	OPTION 1	OPTION 2	OPTION 3
AMOUNT OF THE FUND	100	100	100
LOAN AMOUNT	10	10	10
GUARANTEE COVERAGE RATIO	0.8	0.8	0.5
LEVERAGE	3	2	3
ACCOUNTING PROVISION	60	40	60
NUMBER OF LOANS GUARANTEED	37.5	25	60
VOLUME OF LOANS GUARANTEED	375	250	600

DOI: 10.1057/9781137378477.0013

The financial crisis has accentuated the importance of guarantee funds to increase access to credit for businesses. Banks and financial intermediaries will be more inclined to provide financing knowing that, in case of default, part of its risk will be covered by the guarantee fund. In Europe, there are several countries offering guarantee schemes devoted to the audiovisual industry; of some relevance are the guarantee funds established in France and Spain – based on public-private partnership – and in Germany where each federal State has a public guarantee bank aimed at facilitating lending to SMEs.[22]

For banks and regulated intermediaries, there is one more reason to take advantage of the guarantee funds: the prudential supervision rules they comply with, known as "Basel rules". They require the intermediaries to set aside regulatory capital in relation to the riskiness of the assets they have in their balance sheet. The more risky are the assets, the more capital is required. Banking and financial intermediaries, therefore, are reluctant to provide very risky loans as they demand greater volume of capital. When the loans are covered by collaterals, the percentage of covered loan shall not be reckoned on the purposes of capital absorption. To this end, however, it is important that the guarantee fund is Basel compliant. The Basel rules, in fact, lay down in detail the types of guarantees that are valid for the purposes of capital relief and modes of operation that the guarantee fund must comply with.

A greater involvement of financial intermediaries in the audiovisual market, therefore, necessarily requires the establishment of Basel compliant guarantee funds that can protect intermediaries from excessive exposure to credit risk. These guarantee funds are regarded as useful tools to compensate the lack, on the part of the audiovisual companies, of real guarantees eligible for the purposes of prudential supervision and capital absorption, allowing an easier access to credit for such companies and an easier risk management for financial intermediaries. It was the reason for the establishment of a guarantee fund promoted by the European Commission under the Creative Europe Programme and managed by the EIF, in favour of all the cultural industries. Such a Fund may be used in conjunction with national funds and adapted to the different financing structures used by financial intermediaries in the industry. An increased use of guarantee funds from the national authorities not only favours the leverage of public resources but would be a key lever to stimulate greater involvement of private investors in the audiovisual industry.

DOI: 10.1057/9781137378477.0013

This is also the case of tax incentives, which may be seen as an efficient tool to attract funds on capital markets. In Europe, several countries have introduced fiscal incentives for the audiovisual industry; most of them are intended for producers and distributors, but there are few also devoted to external investors.[23] When dedicated to private investors, fiscal benefits may act as a leverage tool for corporations and financial intermediaries willing to invest in the industry; investment funds may make use of fiscal advantage to promote private funding, while banks are encouraged to combine credit facilities with direct investments.

Any form of fiscal benefit, as well as any public guarantee scheme, has to respect state aid rules; within this legal framework, European countries should promote the implementation of guarantee funds and tax relief measures also aiming at a stronger complementarity with the traditional and incoming financial supports offered by the European Union.

Notes

1 The completion guarantor may also *take over* the film production.

2 For example, insurance on the main cast and the director; or insurance on the certainty of legal rights of a movie script.

3 On average, a completion bond contract requires from the producer a financial commitment of about 5–6% of the total budget of the production.

4 Other two effects of credit risk are the *opportunity cost effect* and the *sale loss effect*, but they do not assume great importance in the audiovisual industry, given the lack of a secondary market for loans.

5 The PD is defined as the mean value of loss distribution for a specific loan category; the LGD is the effective loss and it is calculated as the expected loss rate in percentage of the recovery rate (1-recovery rate).

6 This is particularly true for those intermediaries subject to Basel II and Basel III capital requirements.

7 Examples of banks active in Baujard et al. (2009).

8 For example the LIBOR (London Interbank Offered Rate).

9 The gap financed is usually 10–15% of the budget; the so called "super gap" is around 30% of the total budget: see Baujard et al. (2009).

10 The margin usually acceptable for the banks is of about 200–300% of the amount that is supposed to be granted.

11 Such a *fee* may amount up to 10% of the budget.

12 The average amount of a typical single film financing is around $3–5 million with an average duration of two years (Société Générale 2006).

DOI: 10.1057/9781137378477.0013

13 The average amount of a typical discounting credit facility is around $15–20 million with an average duration of five years. The average amount of a typical film slate financing is around $35 million with an average duration of 18–60 months (Société Générale 2006).
14 In Italy, BNP Paribas offers a special "leasing movie product" through its leasing firm Locafit.
15 Among others, Leone (2006).
16 Usually, the first instalment is much higher than others (paid on a monthly basis) and amounts to 10% of the overall value of the leasing.
17 And so it must have been already funded with other resources.
18 (La Torre M. 2006)
19 The ticked linked bond has an average maturity of 12–18 months (Société Générale 2006).
20 See La Torre M., Mango F., 2011
21 See La Torre (2013).
22 In France the IFCIC (Institute for Financing Cinema and Cultural Industries) is 49% owned by the State and 51% by several commercial banks; in Spain the Audiovisual Mutual Guarantee Society was founded by the Ministry of Culture and the Audiovisual Producers' Rights Management Association (EGEDA). For more details, see: Baujard et al. (2009), http://www.ifcic.eu; http://www.egeda-us.com/Egeda_AudiovisualSGR.asp.
23 Among others, the UK and Italy.

DOI: 10.1057/9781137378477.0013

OPEN

9

The Road Ahead: A Financial Platform for the Audiovisual Industry

Abstract: *The audiovisual industry, in particular the European market, lies behind in terms of evolution of financial dynamics, as well as organization and management of the firms operating in the business. National and EU institutions are currently engaged in an effort to reform the whole audiovisual industry focusing their attention mainly on market dynamics, although they are also seeking to develop a regulatory framework for public measures to support the industry. Financial markets can play a significant role in fostering the audiovisual industry. The chapter proposes a financial platform specifically dedicated to the audiovisual industry, able to combine the needs of the operators and financial intermediaries alike; the chapter describes goals, players, financial instruments and services to be provided by the financial platform.*

La Torre, Mario. *The Economics of the Audiovisual Industry: Financing TV, Film and Web.* Basingstoke: Palgrave Macmillan, 2014. DOI: 10.1057/9781137378477.0014.

 DOI: 10.1057/9781137378477.0014

9.1 The background

The financial dynamics of the audiovisual business are strongly affected by the nature of the products and the production process. Given the cultural nature of audiovisual products, public institutions have traditionally been the major funders of the industry. In Europe, the cultural exception has been, and still is, the principle applied by EU member countries to grant public funds to audiovisual firms.

Audiovisual products are prototype assets by definition; such an intrinsic characteristic makes it very difficult to predict their commercial success and, therefore, estimate the revenues they are able to generate. Moreover, the production of prototype products exposes producers to specific business and process risks. External funders, therefore, are faced with critical issues when assessing the profitability of their investments and risks.

All this explains how, to this day, financing for the audiovisual industry revolves around a model that identifies the actors of the production chain as the industry's funders and public institutions as support parties covering an important part of production budgets.

Yet, opening to capital markets has become an unavoidable necessity for the industry. On one hand, the reduced availability of public funds results in an increasingly marginal role played by national and super-national forms of support to cover production budgets; on the other hand, the decline in advertising revenues – due both to the economic crisis and increasing competition between traditional and new media – has weakened the role of TV broadcasters as important financial backers of the production chain.

A greater involvement of financial intermediaries, and increased use of capital markets, combined with a revised supporting role played by public institutions, are mandatory for the creation of a new and much-needed financial model for the audiovisual industry; one that should be urgently implemented. It is, therefore, necessary to determine the correct conditions to start this innovation process in a harmonious way and establish the direction it should take.

9.2 The great expectations of audiovisual firms

From an economic point of view, each market should be analysed considering both the demand and supply side. Hence, it seems reasonable to start from a fundamental question: what are the expectations of

DOI: 10.1057/9781137378477.0014

the audiovisual industry from the financial system? As a matter of fact, should such expectations not be met, the union between the audiovisual sector and finance would not go very far. Access to capital markets means access to credit and equity sources of funds, yet this condition is not enough to meet the financial requirements of the audiovisual industry. In fact, the funds provided through financial channels must possess some indispensable characteristics for the harmonious development of the firms in the sector. This need translates mainly in the necessity of finding resources in a timely manner and with volumes consistent with production budgets and their financial gaps; moreover, financial costs must reflect the risks related to the rating of the firms or the single projects financed. With regard to the loans and debt instruments, then, the mitigation forms required by lenders must be physiological with the nature of the production process, as well as the specific features of audiovisual firms; the latter, in fact, usually do not own traditional collaterals but intangible assets represented by the exploitation rights on their products. Finally, equity must ensure the financial support needed within governance models that take into account the specific nature of the sector; in this perspective, it is essential, for financial investors, to find a balance between direct involvement in the companies' operations and interferences that could affect the technical-artistic production process.

9.3 The great expectations of financial intermediaries and investors

For financial intermediaries, and banks in particular, financing audiovisual firms presents two critical points: the first one is related to the restrictions established by their internal regulations aimed at ensuring sound and prudent management; the second can be referred to the need of operating following prudential regulatory provisions. In particular, the supervisory regulations under the Basel agreements determine a cost-opportunity of lending that increases the higher the risk of the single credit exposure.

These considerations let us foresee two extreme and alternative scenarios: the first one is characterized by the exclusion of the audiovisual firms from the group of clients deemed to be reliable and creditworthy by lenders; the second scenario envisages a collaboration between

DOI: 10.1057/9781137378477.0014

financial intermediaries and audiovisual firms to create specific financial engineering and models for credit risk assessment aimed at avoiding a penalizing treatment of the loans granted to the subjects operating in this business.

The need for financial engineering able to provide credit mitigation tools is evident not just on the credit market but also in regard to access to capital markets.

9.4 Homework

Financial intermediaries and audiovisual firms should collaborate to define a possible model for the evaluation of the firms operating in the business and their single projects. Both parties have specific interests in doing so; audiovisual firms in seeking alternative financing instruments; financial intermediaries and investors in entering a new market. In spite of the afore-mentioned risks and criticalities, in fact, the audiovisual represents an appealing market for institutional or retail investors. The prototype nature of audiovisual products, and the link between their commercial potential and the response from the public, translate in their capacity to generate revenues regardless of traditional market trends and economic cycles. Following a traditional portfolio logic, this element facilitates the diversification of the investments. Moreover, in spite of a greater volatility of returns, the audiovisual industry may produce very interesting profits, sometimes far higher than the market average.

A convergence process between the audiovisual industry and financial markets must necessarily rely on a pro-active and strong collaboration between financial intermediaries and firms operating in the business. The former, in compliance with their supervisory regulations, should implement new rating models specifically dedicated to audiovisual firms and examine new financial instruments able to reduce exposure to risk.

On the other hand, audiovisual firms should introduce efficient administrative and management criteria in their operations, providing transparent information in order to allow for an accurate evaluation of their products and balance sheets by the financial intermediaries and the market, and also a correct estimate of the risk-return trade off. This is the only way for them to gain the trust of markets and establish long-term and profitable relationships with investors.

DOI: 10.1057/9781137378477.0014

9.5 A financial platform for the audiovisual industry

However, the path outlined cannot be left only to the initiative of the single operators. It is necessary to envisage a systemic effort able to promote measures for the creation of a specific financial market dedicated to the audiovisual industry; such action can be supported and promoted by sector institutions and government policies dedicated to culture.

The financial system is made of different markets; each one of them is characterized by the presence of specialized operators and intermediaries, has its own regulations and specific infrastructures and uses tailor-made financial instruments. The union between finance and audiovisual industry, therefore, cannot dispense from adopting a specialized financial platform.

The urgency to overcome a clear financial crisis of the audiovisual industry has prompted operators to set short-term policies and seek solutions that, being out of the economic context, are likely to result in isolated and ineffective efforts. This is the case of all the actions aimed at raising significant amount of funds from capital markets. Two kinds of problems arise here, though. First of all, the history of finance has taught us that the evolution of financial models always involves a migration from bank-oriented to market-oriented credit systems. It would seem unusual to reverse this pattern for the audiovisual industry, as financial markets cannot be built without first developing credit markets. Banks, in fact, have always played a strategic role in the relationships with the industry: the direct relationships established with firms allow banks to develop skills and know-how needed to assess their clients, production processes and reference markets. The consolidation of the relationships with the clientele in different moments of the production chain allows selecting with accuracy the financial and economic variables to be monitored over time and facilitates the preparation of data bases that can help build and estimate important benchmarks for the sector. Also following such parameters, institutional investors could develop accurate and effective asset management models. A market such as the audiovisual, devoid of specific credit risk evaluation models, could hardly support, with continuity and profit, in an early development stage, initiatives relying on capital markets. Secondly, the investment fund model generally implies involving private investors, besides institutional backers. In this case, any negative performance could soon drive away an important pool of investors, as well as raise

DOI: 10.1057/9781137378477.0014

issues related to the disclosure of risks inherent to the financial instruments placed with the retail customers, which were already experimented by the financial system during the last financial crisis.

A specific financial platform dedicated to the audiovisual industry, able to combine the needs of the operators and financial intermediaries alike, would allow for a gradual passage from a form of indirect intermediation to a more developed direct assisted intermediation.

However, this passage requires a strategic and systemic vision, as well as a number of coordinated actions. Audiovisual production is characterized by a decomposed, yet integrated chain: from pre-production to marketing, each phase features specific economic-financial dimensions that partially interact with other stages.

It is necessary, in the first place, to imagine a platform built on a network system composed of various financial intermediaries, each specialized and able to act on one or more phases of the production process (Figure 9.1).

Assessment of the single projects and the forms of their financial coverage, analysis of mitigation tools and the most suitable covenants for single credit lines, provision of guarantees and insurance coverage, evaluation of the firms' assets and libraries of exploitation rights, rating

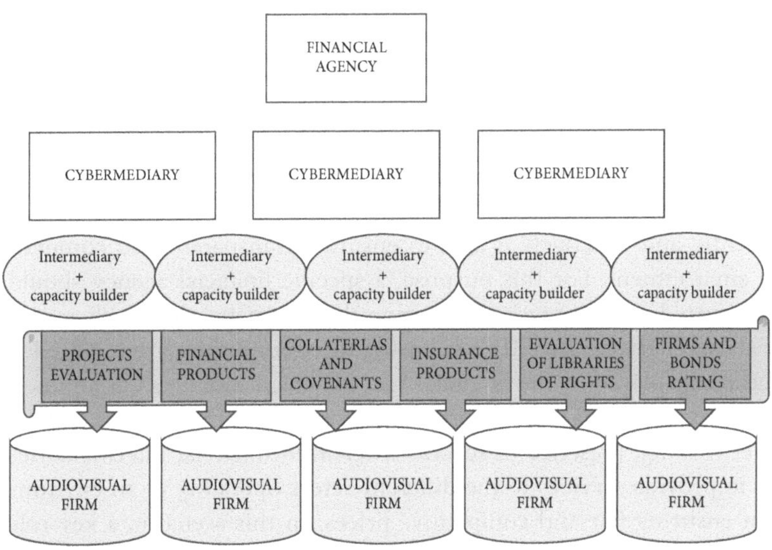

FIGURE 9.1 *A financial platform for the audiovisual industry*

DOI: 10.1057/9781137378477.0014

assignment, support and assistance services provided to firms to access the capital markets, are just some of the specialized functions that should be offered by a financial platform dedicated to the audiovisual industry. On the other hand, the financial dynamics of the audiovisual production process involve multiple and intense interactions all along the production chain. Just think about the relationships between production, distribution and retail. Financial support, therefore, should follow this double nature of the production process: specialization and integration. If, on one hand, the different financial intermediaries need to develop specific expertise, justified by the different operational skills that they must provide and fair risk allocation; on the other hand, the financial system should meet the demand of the single operators without losing track of the unity of the production process.

For such reason, a dedicated platform must ensure to the single financial intermediaries the possibility of evaluating their support within the entire production chain, as well as other dynamics of the single projects or firms. Financial intermediaries must, therefore, be supported in their activity by institutions able to integrate decomposed production processes.

In this regard, it must be noted that some of the most innovative financial markets are experimenting the birth of new intermediaries able to integrate unrelated production processes and operate through the use of multimedia platforms. Such intermediaries have been named "cyber-mediaries", acting as intelligent service providers for the whole production chain. Audiovisual cyber-mediaries should offer their services – also through multimedia channels – by acting as connectors between the industry and specialized financial intermediaries for each project or firm assisted. A similar network, though, can only work efficiently and effectively if able to ensure a transparent and competitive environment. For this purpose, a specific financial agency should be entrusted with the task of ensuring that the network complies with the above characteristics. The following three conditions are required: a neutral role played by the financial agency, which should act as an intelligent coordinator of the network; cyber-mediaries limiting their activity to networking; presence of several specialized financial intermediaries able to provide services to the different actors operating in an environment ensuring fair and competitive prices. In this scenario, a key role is played by capacity-building providers, i.e. those specialized subjects operating at national and pan-European levels, that can assist banks

DOI: 10.1057/9781137378477.0014

and financial intermediaries in entering the market and developing the appropriate skill to manage the business efficiently.

9.6 Policy recommendations

The audiovisual industry, in particular the European market, lies behind in terms of evolution of financial dynamics, as well as organization and management of the firms operating in the business. National and EU institutions are currently engaged in an effort to reform the whole audiovisual and cultural sector. EU Institutions and national public bodies have focussed their attention mainly on strategic and market dynamics, although they are also seeking to develop a regulatory framework for public measures to support the industry. In Europe, the new *Cinema Communication* and the cultural support programme *Creative Europe* share a common objective: to facilitate the transition of the audiovisual industry from artisanal to industrial market, while protecting the authorship and cultural diversity. This is the direction taken by a number of measures aimed at facilitating access to finance for the audiovisual firms – such as the creation of the Guarantee Fund under the programme *Creative Europe*.

In this perspective, a financial platform specifically dedicated to the audiovisual industry would allow conferring to the single, even praiseworthy initiatives, an organic and systemic character. Institutions, therefore, should stimulate the creation of more developed financial infrastructure in order to avoid limiting the single initiatives to an area restricted to a few players. This is a hard but mandatory way to be pursued by the whole audiovisual and cultural industry.

DOI: 10.1057/9781137378477.0014

References

Adam D. (1958) *Les Reactions du Consommateur devant Le Prix*, Sedes, Paris.

Adler T. (2003a) Societe Generale Planning £ 170m Film Fund, *Screen Finance*, 16(4).

—— (2003b) Only One Third of European Features Make a Profit, *Screen Finance*, 16(8).

Baravelli M. (2001) *Lo sviluppo dei sistemi finanziari a rete*, Newfin, Bocconi University, n°3.

Barker R. (2003) Watch the Movie, Skip the IPO, *BusinessWeek*, 15 December.

Basuroy S., Chatterjee S. and Ravid S. A. (2003) How Critical Are Critical Reviews? The Box Office Effects of Film Critics, Star Power, and Budgets, *Marketing*, 67(4), pp. 103–117.

Baujard T., Lauriac M., Robert M. and Cadio S. (2009) *Study on the Role of Banks in the European Film Industry*, Peacefulfish, Media Programme Report, Bruxelles.

Bel G. and Domenech L. (2008) What Influences Advertising Price in Television Channels?: An Empirical Analysis on the Spanish Market, *Journal of Media Economics*, 22(3), pp. 164–183.

Biondi C. (2000) *Controllo e Pianificazione della produzione Audiovisiva*, Dino Audino Editore.

—— (2002) *Come si Produce un Film*, Dino Audino Editore, vol. 3 edn. 4.

Burrows H. and Ussher K. (2011) *Risky Business*, Demos, London.

Clayton L. and Mason H. (2006) *The Financing of UK Creative Industries SMEs*, BOP & Pembridge, London.

DOI: 10.1057/9781137378477.0015

Committeri G. and La Torre M. (2008) *Agevolazioni fiscali per il cinema*, Quaderni Anica, Rome.

Cones J. W. (1998) *43 Ways to Finance Your Feature Film*, Southern Illinois Press, Carbondale.

Cook M., Earley F., Ketteringham J. and Smith S. (2002) *Losing Interest: How Much Can Consumers Save by Shopping around for Financial Products?*, FSA Occasional paper series 19.

Costabile M. (1992) *Prezzo e consumatore: il ruolo del prezzo nel processo d'acquisto*, Egea, Milano.

Crampes C. and Hollander A. (2005) Product Specification, Multi-Product Screening and Bundling: The Case of Pay TV, *Information Economics and Policy*, 17(1), pp. 35–59.

Dally P., Durandez A., Jimenez L., Pasquale A. and Vidal C. (2002) *The Audiovisual Management Handbook*, Media Business School Publication, Madrid.

DCMS (Department for Culture, Media and Sport) (1998) *Creative industries mapping document*, Creative Task Force, London.

De Bande O. and Chetrit G. (2001) *The European Audiovisual Industry. An Overview*, EIB Sector Papers.

De Vany A. (2004) *Hollywood Economics: How Extreme Uncertainty Shapes the Film Industry.* Rouledge, London.

Demattè C. and Perretti F. (1997) *L'impresa televisiva*, Etaslibri, Milano.

Derecki K. (2004) Learn to Juggle if You Need Film Finance: Production Budgets, *Financial Times*, 7 September.

Doshi L. and Krauss J. (2010) Predicting Movie Prices Through Dynamic Social Network Analysis, *Procedia Social and Behavioral Sciences*, 2, pp. 6423–6433.

Driver T.C. (2002) In Facing a Clear & Present Ranger Are We Equal to the Sum of All Fears, *The Business of Film*, Analysis –Financing, November, Mifed Special Issue.

European Commission (2012) *Report on Measures to Protect and Promote the Diversity of Cultural Expression in the Framework of the 2005 UNESCO Convention*, Commission Staff Working Document, C (2012) 3186, Brussels.

—— (2010a) *Green Paper on Cultural and Creative Industries*, Brussels.

—— (2010b) *European Competitiveness Report*, Brussels.

European Commission Cinema Communication: 2013/C 332/01.

Eliashberg J. and Shugan S. (1997) Film Critics: Influencers or Predictors, *Journal of Marketing*, 61(2), pp. 68–78.

DOI: 10.1057/9781137378477.0015

ESSnet_culture: Final Report 212, Luxembourg, http://ec.europa.eu/culture/library/reports/ess-net-report_en.pdf

EU. (2010) Audiovisual Media Service Directive, Directive 2010/13/EU.

European Audiovisual Observatory, *Yearbooks*, Strasbourg . (several years)

European Audiovisual Observatory, *Yearbooks* (2014) On-demand Audiovisual Markets in the European Union, EU.

F.Ar.M. (2006) Master in Film Art Management, "La Sapienza University of Rome", Internal documents.

Foutz N. Z. and Jank W. (2010) Prerelease Demand Forecasting for Motion Pictures Using Functional Shape Analysis of Virtual Stock Markets, *Marketing Science*, 29(3), pp. 568–579.

Gabor A. and Granger C. W. J. (1961) On the Price Consciousness of Consumers, *Applied Statistics*, 10(November), pp. 170–188.

—— (1965) The Pricing of New Products, *Scientific Business*, 3(August), pp. 141–150.

Gangemi G., Marzulli A. and Zambardino B. (2013) Lo Scenario della produzione e distribuzione di web series, study committed by RAI Radiotelevisione Italiana, Icom, Roma.

Godes D., Ofek E. and Sarvary M. (2009) Content vs. Advertising: The Impact of Competition on Media Firm Strategy, *Marketing Science*, INFORMS, 28(1), pp. 20–35.

Hancock C. and Wistreich N. (2004) *Get Your Film Funded: UK Film Finance Guide*, Shooting People Press.

HKU (2010) *The Entrepreneurial Dimension of the Cultural and Creative Industries*, Hogeschool vor de Kunsten Utrecht, Utrecht.

Holden J. (2006) *Cultural Value and the Crisis of Legitimacy*, Demos, London.

IDEA Consult (2012) *Study on the Financing Needs and the Use of Additional Financing Instruments in the Arts*, study commissioned by the Flemish regional agency Arts & Heritage.

—— (2013) *Survey on Access to Finance for Cultural and Creative Sectors*, study commissioned by the European Commission.

IMCA (2001) *Identification et Evaluation des Flux Economiques et Financiérs du Cinéma en Europe et Comparaison avec le Modéle Américain*; Report to the European Commission, Study n° DG EAC/34/01.

DOI: 10.1057/9781137378477.0015

Jacoby J.and Kaplan L. (1972) *The Components of Perceived Risk*, Proceedings from Third Annual Conference. Association for Consumer Research: University of Chicago, pp. 382–393.

Joshi A. M. and Hanssens D. M. (2009) Movie Advertising and Stock Market Valuation of Studios: A Case of "Great Expectations?", *Marketing Science*, 28(2), pp. 239–250.

Kaplan L. B., Zybillo G. J. and Jacoby J. (1974) Components of Perceived Risk in Product Purchase: Cross-validation, *Journal of Applied Psychology*, 59(June), pp. 287–291.

Katona G. (1977) *Psychological Analysis of Economic Behavior*, Greenwood Press, Westport, Conn.

KEA (2006) *The Economy of Culture in Europe*, study commissioned by European Commission.

—— (2010a) *Analysis of the Financing Needs, Best Practices and Opportunities for the Creative Sector in Europe* , ECCE Innovation, Nantes Métropole.

—— (2010b) *Promoting Investment in the Cultural and Creative Sector: Financing Needs, Trends and Opportunities*; Report prepared for ECCE Innovation – Nantes Métropole.

Kind H. J., Nilssen T. and Sorgard L. (2009) Business Models for Media Firms: Does Competition Matter for How They Raise Revenue?, *Marketing Science*, 28(6), pp. 1112–1128.

La Torre M. (2003a) *Banks in the European Film Industry: Financial Techniques and Risks*, paper presented to the annual conference of the European Association of University Teachers of Banking and Finance, Dublin.

—— (2003b) Economia e dinamiche finanziarie del cinema, *Bancaria*, n°10.

—— (2003c) Le Banche nel cinema: un modello di gestione del credito cinematografico, *Bancaria*, n°12.

—— (2004) Per un parco finanziario del cinema, *Banche e Banchieri*, n°5.

—— (2006a) *La Finanza del Cinema* (edited by), Bancaria Editrice.

—— (2006b) La finanza del cinema: Spielberg e la lezione del mercato americano, *Bancaria*, n°12.

—— (2013) Social Lending in Europe: Structures, Regulation and Pricing Models, in *Banking and Financial Institutions* (ed.) Juan Fernández de Guevara Radoselovics, José Pastor Monsálvez., Palgrave Macmillan, London.

DOI: 10.1057/9781137378477.0015

La Torre M. and Mango F. (2011) "Asset-Backed Securitization and Financial Stability: the Downgrading Delay Effect " In *Banks Performance Risk and Firm Financing*, P. Molyneaux, Palgrave Macmillan.

La Torre M. and Vento G. (2006) Microfinance, Palgrave Macmillan, London.

Lambin J. J. (2000) *Marketing strategico e operativo*, McGraw-Hill, Milan.

Leo S. (2009) *Il pricing nel credito cinematografico,* paper presented to the ADEIMF annual conference, Palermo.

Leone C. (2006) I finanziamenti sul mercato dei capitali, in *La Finanza del Cinema* (ed.) La Torre M., Bancaria Editrice.

Levison L. (1998) *Filmmakers and Financing. Business Plan for Independents* (*Second Edition*), Local Press.

Monroe, K. B. (1971) Measuring Price Thresholds by Psychophysics and Latitudes of Acceptance, *Journal of Marketing Research*, 8(November), pp. 460–464.

Nagle T. and Holden R. K. (1994) *Strategy and Tactics of Pricing*, Pearson US Imports & Philes, Welwyn Garden City.

Neumann P. and Appelgren C. (2007) *The Fine Art of Co-Production*, Neumann Publishing.

O'Brien D. (2010) *Measuring the Value of Culture: A Report to the Department of Culture, Media and Sport*, AHRC/ESRC Placement Fellow, December.

O'Brien S. (2002) Completion Bonds Become Gaming Buzzword, *Screen Finance*, 20 November.

Ottaviani M. (2000) *Economics of Advice*, Mimeo, Department of Economics and ELSE, University College London.

Porter M. E. (1983) *La strategia competitive*, Bologna, Edizioni della Tipografia Compositori.

Sawhney M. S. and Eliashberg J. (1996) A Parsimonious Model for Forecasting Gross Box-Office Revenues of Motion Pictures, *Marketing Science*, 15(2), pp. 113–131.

Société Générale (2006) *Internal Documents* prepared for the F.Ar.M – Master in Film Art Management, "La Sapienza University of Rome".

Song P., Sun J. and Feng K. (2011) *Research of the Content Product Pricing Method Based on Exploitation of Digital Media Assets*, International Conference on Management and Service Science.

Stoetzel J. (1954) Le prix comme limité, in Reynaud P.L. *La psicologie economique*, Libraire Marcel Riviere et Cie, Paris.

DOI: 10.1057/9781137378477.0015

Throsby D. (2001) *Economics and Culture*, Cambridge: Cambridge University Press.

UNESCO (2009) *UNESCO Framework for Cultural Statistics*, UNESCO Institute for Statistic, Montreal, Canada.

—— (2005*) UNESCO Convention on the Protection and Promotion of the Diversity of Cultural Expression*, Paris.

Valdani E. (1986) *Marketing Strategico*, Etas Libri, Milano.

Wolinsky A. (1983) Prices as Signals of Product Quality, *The Review of Economic Studies*, 50(4), pp. 647– 658.

Yoo M. K. and Lim S. (2010) Price Forecasting Model of the FPD Market with Existing Technological Variance – Case: Global FPD TV Market, *Expert System with Application*, 37(9), pp. 6459–6469.

Zeithaml V. A. (1988) Consumer Perceptions of Price, Quality and Value: A Means-End Model and Synthesis of Evidence, *Journal of Marketing*, 52, pp. 2–22.

Zufryden F. (1996) Linking Advertising to Box-office Performance of New Film Releases – A Marketing Planning Model, *Journal of Advertising Research*, 36(4), pp. 29–41.

DOI: 10.1057/9781137378477.0015

Index

DOI: 10.1057/9781137378477.0016

DOI: 10.1057/9781137378477.0016

DOI: 10.1057/9781137378477.0016

DOI: 10.1057/9781137378477.0016

DOI: 10.1057/9781137378477.0016

DOI: 10.1057/9781137378477.0016

DOI: 10.1057/9781137378477.0016

DOI: 10.1057/9781137378477.0016

The manufacturer's authorised representative in the EU is Springer Nature Customer Service Centre GmbH, Europaplatz 3, 69115 Heidelberg, Germany. If you have any concerns regarding our products, please contact ProductSafety@springernature.com

Printed and bound by CPI Group (UK) Ltd, Croydon, CR0 4YY

12/08/2026

02194516-0003